BLACK
WRITERS
MATTER

BLACK
WRITERS
MATTER

edited by
WHITNEY
FRENCH

 University of Regina Press

Printed and bound in Canada at Imprimerie Gauvin. The text of this book is printed on 100% post-consumer recycled paper with earth-friendly vegetable-based inks.

Cover design: Duncan Campbell, University of Regina Press
Text design: John van der Woude, JVDW Designs
Copy editor: Marionne Cronin
Proofreader: Kristine Douaud

Library and Archives Canada Cataloguing in Publication

Black writers matter / edited by Whitney French.

Issued in print and electronic formats. ISBN 978-0-88977-616-6 (softcover).— ISBN 978-0-88977-617-3 (PDF).—ISBN 978-0-88977-618-0 (HTML)

1. Creative nonfiction, Canadian (English). 2. Canadian literature (English)— Black Canadian authors. 3. Canadian prose literature (English)—21st century. I. French, Whitney, 1987-, editor

PS8235.B53B53 2019   C810.8′0896071   C2018-906025-5   C2018-906026-3

10 9 8 7 6 5 4 3

University of Regina Press, University of Regina
Regina, Saskatchewan, Canada, S4S 0A2
tel: (306) 585-4758 fax: (306) 585-4699
web: www.uofrpress.ca

U OF R PRESS

We acknowledge the support of the Canada Council for the Arts for our publishing program. We acknowledge the financial support of the Government of Canada. / Nous reconnaissons l'appui financier du gouvernement du Canada. This publication was made possible with support from Creative Saskatchewan's Book Publishing Production Grant Program.

CONTENTS

ACKNOWLEDGEMENTS

Give thanks to the Creator, first and foremost. I'd also like to acknowledge my ancestors, known and unknown; I dedicate any writing I create to you. And to acknowledge my literary guides—those walking this Earth and those who've transitioned to other realms. You left artifacts of writing to remind me of my humanity. To my parents, Angella and Lascelle French, for their unwavering support. Every story presented in the anthology, I picture you both reading it. You two are my compass. So much love to my sisters Carla and Nicolette, who are the most hard-core cheerleaders a girl could ask for. And to my best friend Anita Abbasi, who holds so much emotional space for me, always.

I'd like to thank the University of Regina Press and Bruce Walsh for presenting this exciting project to me. Much love to Scott Fraser, my anthology's 'midwife,' endless gratitude to my mentor David Chariandy whose generosity and encouragement not only helped me through early developmental stages but also allowed me to focus on the heart of what this work truly is. A thousand thanks to my P.C.O. crew for feedback on early versions of the introduction: Gwen Benaway, Alicia Elliot, Kim Sənklip Harvey, Rebecca Salazar Leon, Carrianne Leung, Canisia Lubrin, Minelle Mahtani, Eli Tareq, Cason Sharpe, Natalie Wee, and Jenny Heijun Wills. Respect and thanks to M. NourbeSe Philip for sage advice around writing and anthology work. Thank you to Sommer Blackman for reminding me to fight for what I deserve. Respect, love, and inspiration to Dawn Dumont, Night Kinistino, Lindsay Knight, Erica Violet Lee,

Nickita Longman, and Sylvia McAdam. Miigwetch to Jamaias DaCosta, who helped immensely with coordinating the "My Ancestors' Wildest Dream" interviews. A heart-filled thanks to Dr. Afua Cooper for making time to write the foreword. To Lily Quan for recommending Black writers up north. Also big up Dalton Higgins for being a sounding board for so many frazzled ideas in my head. So much gratitude to Angela Wright for ranting alongside me during the most frustrating phases of this anthology. To my literary soul sister Sheniz Janmohamed, who forever surprises me with her love, verve, and passion for life.

Thank you to anyone on social media who spread the word about the call-out and thought that this project was worth sharing with their networks. This anthology wouldn't have happened without you. Honest. And of course, to all the contributors for trusting me with your writing. I hope I honoured your stories. You all inspire me so.

And give thanks to my brain...for not exploding.

PERFORMING MIRACLES: BLACK WRITERS MATTER

— Dr. Afua Cooper —

Whitney French has performed a small miracle by bringing these stories in *Black Writers Matter* into a single anthology. This collection stands out from previous literary anthologies in that all the stories are written from the first-person perspective, and thus are extremely personal. And yet they are simultaneously political because Black writing by its very nature is political.

These voices range across age and space. This collection is a rich potpourri, a jambalaya of Black Canadian voices. These stories include memoirs, interviews, questionnaires, meditations, and other creative non-fiction pieces. The writers are high school and university students, artists, academics, cab drivers, poets, dreamers, lawyers, and community workers. They come from diverse parts of the Black Diaspora, but they and their families now converge and live in Canada, whether it's for a few decades or a few centuries.

As I read each story, the James Baldwin quote that "to be a Negro...and to be relatively conscious is to be in a rage almost all the time" resounded in my head. All the writers in the collection touch a place of rage in their writing as they narrate, chronicle, and relate their experiences as

Black, gendered, and sexualized individuals living in different places in Canada. In fact, as shown by Angela Wright's story "The Place That Is Supposed To Be Safe," by the time some Black children are in grade six they experience rage on a daily basis.

It was a privilege to be asked to write this foreword. As I read the pages, I realized that I was holding sacred text. Reading these stories gave me both joy and grief. Laughter broke out unexpectedly as I read Dwight Phillip Morgan's "Becoming a Shark," as he cycled uphill to Whistler, BC, asking himself "What am I doing here?" as he tried to prove his Canadianness. I was moved to tears as I read Rowan McCandless "Hunger Games," a startling and intensely personal piece on anorexia and bulimia, and Rachel Zellers's "Shame and the Kinship of Sexual Violence" that speaks to inter-generation shame and sexual trauma within Black families. Brandon Wint stills the breath with his beautiful meditation on being Black, a poet, and disabled. And Meshama Eyob Austin, on the cusp of her glorious woman-hood, through the help of her mother, discovers her voice, and challenges a school teacher who refuses to attend to the complaints of racism from her students. And who would not be moved by the image of Mary Louise McCarthy walking through abandoned cemeteries in New Brunswick, looking for evidence of her Black ancestors that white society sought to bury forever? We are doubly blessed with the wisdom of the s/ages from seasoned writer H. Nigel Thomas, who reminds us that for many Black writers literature has always served as a liberatory tool. Scott Fraser urges us to remember that racism is really white people's problem because they created it, but he also advises that we must always, echoing Baldwin, live our life as if we have a right to it. Kyla Farmer brilliantly uses a multidisci-plinary approach to tell a story of her African Nova Scotian paternal roots.

A cab driver is reminded of a locale in Ethiopia when he lands at a village in British Columbia. And by doing so links African memories with the new ones he is creating in the Diaspora. And this is one of the geniuses of this collection. How often do we hear the narratives that Black cabbies have to tell? They are cab drivers after all. They should just drive. But Whitney French thought otherwise, and in her decision to interview a Black cabbie, a new world is revealed.

If there is a unifying theme in this anthology, it is the pain and burden of anti-black racism. Each writer tells us in a different way how painful it is for them as they realize, sometimes abruptly, sometimes over a long period, that white Canadian society views Black people as inferior beings and the damage to Black psyches and bodies that this view has wrought. But as Alice Walker grasps: we carry within us the medicine for our pain.* And that is what *Black Writers Matter* does: it presents the pain, mourning, and sorrow, but each story carries within it its own medicine, its own balm, its own antidote. And that is part of the small miracle that French has performed.

Each writer draws on their own lineage of the past and steers their vision to champion and create a revolutionary afrofuture. And so we write. These writings come out of our interior spaces, our humanity and loves writ large; but the dialectic is ever present. In the outer world: we march, protest, revolt, rebel, rage, sing, drum, firebun, and fight like raas.

These stories remind me of my own lineage, history, trajectory, immigrant experience, and coming into my own as a writer. I smile as I hear some of the writers, like French, talking about their own hesitant journey toward embracing the writer within themselves, and coming upon that stunning realization that their writing *matters*. French is to be commended for giving this gift of an anthology to the world.

Afua Cooper
Halifax, Nova Scotia
August 2018

---

* Alice Walker, Foreword to Zora Neale Hurston's *Barracoon: The Story of the Last "Black Cargo,"* New York: HarperCollins Publishers, 2018, xii.

INTRODUCTION
THE ACT OF **GATHERING**

— *Whitney French* —

I am six years old:
tracing the rings of a tree stump, a crass cut, its former self a hazard, being so close to the playground and so close to a phone pole. My fingers follow the rings of the creamy sapwood, counting an uncountable number for a kindergartener, whispering guesses of the tree's age. The pith is cracked and black, a contrast to the smooth texture of the inner flesh, all the while the outer bark rubs against my socked foot.

As a small-town Black kid wanting to write, surviving off the works of Toni Morrison and James Baldwin and in later years M. NourbeSe Philip and George Elliott Clarke with vision and scope and subject matter far beyond my understanding, I was granted strength and love from Black people through words.

And so my mantra throughout the building of this anthology is: every day, everyday. The rhythmic duality grounds me. The first 'every day' is a constant reminder that I am and will always be Black, every day. My blackness doesn't change, it doesn't grow, it doesn't fade. It is my everyday and so I must meditate on my relationship to that reality and to the works that I come in contact with constantly.

The second 'everyday' is a reminder of the people, and a reminder to self to cultivate community. Parents, children, workers, teachers, lovers, dreamers—everyday people are the soul-blood of *Black Writers Matter*. Authors will be forever canonized, but who will document everyone else?

I am six years old:
scanning the world around me, the bigness of the playground, which is near the centre of town, which is a town hugged tightly by a canal, which is a canal that is wrapped around a marsh, one of many that make up the green belt in Southern Ontario, which is of a territory that is not mine. It hardly feels half-mine. I'm scanning the world around me, looking for colours that match me (yesterday I used up the all black and brown and orange crayons in the mesh basket), colours like this dark pith or this burnt almond leaf or this wing tip of a sparrow or this nut brown of an acorn—that matches me.

The weight of an anthology is to be acknowledged and honoured but it is also a form of canonizing, which by its very nature includes and excludes. My intention is that this collection—far from any definitive— acts as an invitation to read, share, and tell stories of Black narratives that are close to the bone. I am reminding myself to carve space for unique tellers, overlooked tellers. The process of interviewing, blog-hunting, and excavating stories in unexpected places was integral. The anthology as a text acts as a gathering and actions me to gather.

I am six years old:
collecting bits of things that I can see in me, that elicit temporary com- fort, but all my gatherings of colours and phrases and images from TV, from strangers, from friends, from family, fall flat against the starkness of white-Bradford.

Born without a community of Black folks outside my kin, I've been compulsively collecting and creating communities of colour, and Black communities especially, since leaving my hometown. I am compelled to look at the ways stories ravel and unravel through time and even in spite of time. Non-linear expression encourages a playfulness, a serious investigation, a more embodied way of dealing with text without chronological predictability and hindrance. I am no longer obsessed with 'accuracy' or the weight of any Eurocentric understandings of 'nonfiction.' Instead, I turn my attention to multiple truths that surface from these tellings and try to expand the very container that we argue, disrupt, challenge, and recreate. This practice generates boundless room to parse out our own personal myths and our own centralized truths.

I am six years old:
make-believing all the things outside of my present reality, blowing up the universe beyond the realm of teachers who do not place value on Black History Month, of friends' parents who think I steal from their homes, or of adults who tell me that slavery "was a good thing" since Black people came to know Jesus Christ as their Lord and Saviour; blowing up the universe beyond the confines of a town so small and so big at the same time.

A part of me wanted this anthology to have the energy of a big dinner where everyone is loosely related, some folks know each other, some do not. We've all come from different places, and all have made long journeys to get here; sitting inside of someone else's experience through the written word.

I am six years old:
listening to my second-grade teacher tell me of a story of how a Black girl from Bradford can become a writer, if she wants to. It is the most impactful story of my life. It is the only thing, the biggest thing, I can gather and it feels mine.
    Fully mine.

The big family dinner thing, I know now, is less about the illusion of unity and more about the immediate and undeniable truths of our stories. Our plainness and extraordinariness. Our mundane disasters and collective devastations. Our stories are our survival and to slap lofty ideals of coherence and conclusiveness would be false, a distancing from 'nonfiction.'

So I invite readers to shift/rattle/augment their understanding of creative nonfiction—which often appears in the form of an essay that proves a point—to a blending of multiple genres. This blending is organically Canadian. A true multiverse of cultures that doesn't ignore systemic oppressions, unlike the branded benevolent multiculturalism we've been fed for far too long.

Maybe it is unfair to say—or too fair to say—that collecting bits of things, gathering, and amassing is a process that feels particular to the Black Canadian experience. By showing our experiences in its multitudes and smashing the monolith, *Black Writers Matter* injects new meaning into the word *diversity*; it harbours a sacredness and an everydayness that offers Black people dignity. Six-year-old Whitney, so desperate for validation, has grown up. I'm not interested in asking people to see our humanity. I'm simply here to celebrate it. Read on, and celebrate alongside me.

Whitney French
Toronto, Ontario
February 2018

EVERYDAY
PEOPLE

WHAT WILL YOU TELL YOUR CHILDREN?

SIMONE MAKEBA DALTON

We were nearly drowned by a sea of blue and white.

Donna, Akeisha, Stephanie, two Crystals, and I. Except there was no sea, but 800 or so uniformed girls dressed in blue-and-white checkered tunics over white short-sleeved shirts. With bobbing and laughing bodies, they rushed out of cramped classrooms from the left, the right, the top, and the bottom, to the lunchtime bell of our primary school.

We could see our principal, Mrs. Daniel, lording over her charges. She looked precarious as ever; her large bottom, cocked high, tested the strength of her stiletto heels. We could hear the competing choruses of "Brown Girl in the Ring" begin as we pressed ourselves against the locked gates of our school. We could also see the busy two-lane carriageway with its rum shops on either side beckoning beyond.

Have you ever seen a rum shop in the daylight? How the cracks in the paint are no longer hidden by the marquee lights? How the patrons spilling out of its doors all wear the same shade of shame across their faces?

We were tall for our ages of nine and ten, though I, at four feet eleven inches, was the shortest of the clique. We often stood with a girlish closeness, shoulder to shoulder, arms at times interlaced. The inherent 'we' disappeared into the singularity of sameness—same two plaits, same bony legs, same prepubescent voice.

Girls were allowed through the school's gates before 3 p.m. on two occasions: to make the Stations of the Cross in May, or with a signed note from a parent. Earlier that day, I had shown Mrs. About-To-Fall-Over my permission slip. The single foolscap sheet was a familiar shade of yellow. It reminded me of corn, just before it's roasted by the lick of red flames from a coal pot. My mother's penmanship defied the faint blue, single-spaced, ruled lines of the page, each cursive letter taller than the next. Her crowning glory, the swooping E.D. of her initials, finished her request. I was to be let out of school that day. My father was taking me to lunch.

There is nothing unusual about a father taking a daughter to lunch. But it was unusual for that father to be mine. Unusual for him to be there, in Trinidad, a place where he was born but did not live. He lived where a Red Rocket takes thousands of people to work, school, and play. Sometimes the faces of those people are twisted in mournful ways. That's how you know it's winter.

I had seen him fewer times than I had blown out candles on my birthday cake. I knew him from Oh Henry! chocolate bars and stuffed animals he left at my grandmother's house. He sometimes brought clothes for me, though they were never quite big enough. Once, he brought a roll of used pens and pencils kept together with a rubber band. I wanted to use the pens in school the next term, even though we weren't allowed to write with ballpoint pens yet.

When he approached the gate, we fanned out like dominos. Donna was the first to speak. Her "that's" became "dais" when she asked, "That's your daddy? He's so handsome!" She was equal parts admiration and awe. Donna's father was always at the dinner table whenever I was invited to share a meal at her house. What might have come across as imposing from his muscular fireman's frame was immediately lost when he laughed. I didn't know a more handsome man at the time.

My father made his way slowly up the broad concrete staircase. He was dressed like a man on holiday. His collared shirt and shorts looked like a matching set, except for the dots of pink flamingo feathers peeking out from behind the palm trees.

The exchange of a few words between him and the security guard at the gate was the only time I had to gather my thoughts. It was decided. I would introduce him as "Dad" since I had never called him "Daddy." The back of my throat tickled with the flutters that were once in the pit of my stomach. Out of the sun, he squinted into the sea of blue and white, looking for the first sign of a life that belonged to him. There he stood for all to see. I suddenly felt free of the secret dash under "Father's Name" on my birth certificate. Someone nudged me forward. "Dad," I called out as I waved shyly.

"There you are!" he said, with his arms open and lips parted wide to reveal a smile. "Are these your friends, Sam?" I forgot to tell the girls that when he says "Sam" he means me; it's the nickname that he decided I should have when I was born. My face grew hot. To recover from my embarrassment, I began to quickly make the rounds, introducing each one of my friends by name. He looked happy and seemed interested in getting to meet the quintet, to experience the easy sum total of my life at the time.

Dad and I crossed the street, past the bars, and headed to a chicken and chips spot of my choice for our lunch date.

———

That was 1991. It is now 2017.

I sit across the dining room table from my father. The half-lit room is filled with the sounds of screeching basketball sneakers and "Defence! Defence!" from his too-loud television. Even the halftime buzzer cannot save the Toronto Raptors from tonight's loss. Outside it's chilly, but sweat runs down the crease of my back. The apartment's thirty-year-old thermostat only registers two temperatures: off and dry-season hot. I turn to watch the near-naked maple tree branches on his balcony as they make tortured shadows against the wall of glass that separates us from the susurration of an evening breeze.

To be deciduous is to "fall away." Maples trees, like the one outside my father's apartment, are reduced to a carpet of fallen leaves when the damp crispness of autumn arrives. I'm not a tree. Through most of the seasons of my life I have longed to fall into my father's stories. To get closer to him. To know him and for him to know me.

I started asking him questions about his life, after my mother's death. I tried to piece together parts of him from a handful of black-and-white photos I saw once, but the gaps remained. Who was the boy at seven, the one dressed for church in knee-length slacks, a short-sleeved shirt, spit-shine Oxfords, and a pair of tall socks? His self-effacing demeanour was quite unlike the womanizer Dad was reputed to be. Then there was the boy who raced clothespin boats in the skim of water that collected under his neighbour's house after the rain. That neighbour happened to be Stokely Carmichael. What was it like to be playmates with a future American Civil Rights leader? Playmates in the way that children become fond of one another when there is one football, one cricket bat, or a single packet of jacks to be shared among all of the households on the street.

I felt the echoes of the choices my father had made, but I had no sense of why those choices were made in the first place.

What I had instead was a composite of stories of my creation. There were scenes punctuated by a lilting voice with pronounced calypso tones over distorted, collect phone calls, and looping signatures of "Love, Dad" in occasional birthday cards sent by airmail.

My mother also authored her own stories about him. She sometimes stopped mid-sentence, interrupting her instruction of a chore or chide. Mouth agape with wonder, her lips snapped back into motion only to say, "Lord, child, you looked like your father just now!" When I asked over and over how she knew she wanted him, to have his baby, my five-foot-nine, statuesque mother always looked nostalgic. "He was good looking and had brains for so," she said with a smile that curled her lips back far enough to reveal two miniscule splices of gold implanted between her teeth. My body had its way of revealing its own tale about my father. For a while, his forehead was my least favourite inheritance.

Sitting in his house, I now know the address and the dwelling it leads to. A veil of mystery is lifted. No longer do I have to fantasize about boats moored outside his bedroom window, as the tide ebbed out to sea. Those were the dreams of a child. This just my father's two-bedroom apartment on Longboat Avenue.

My fingers circle the rim of a glass of rum and Coke on the table in front of me. He's on his second drink, but without the Coke. Instead, the dark molasses colour of the rum is bleached by a splash of water and ice. Tonight he's uncorked a bottle of his fifteen-year-old Eldorado Special Reserve. Our arms cycle through the same motions as if in mime.

I shift in my chair. There is barely enough room for my rib cage to expand, but I make do with the discomfort. I don't want to disturb the disorder of his things. There are piles of open bills, books being read, his toque and two pairs of dollar-store glasses on the table. Soon a meal will be before us—a pot of pelau is on the stove, with pieces of chicken browned by burnt sugar, pillowed by rice and pigeon peas. Like me, the food is different from the fare we shared during those childhood show-and-tell lunches of yesteryear. I'm older, braver, more curious.

On the wall in front of me is a framed newspaper clipping from 1971 with the headline, "Biggest Conference of Blacks In The History of Canada To Be Held In Toronto, Feb 19th." A small photograph of my father is in the frame under the boldfaced, all-capped, black letters. Though the sharpness of the ink print has dulled with age, the prominence of his Afro is not to be mistaken. It is anchored by dark sunglasses; he's been wearing his indoors since long before it became cool in the eighties. The waist-deep photo shows him in a khaki trench coat with a black turtle-neck. His angular cheekbones and nose are in profile, pointed towards his chest and away from the viewing audience as he broods over a sheet of paper. Those are my cheekbones, my nose. I move through the world with his watermark.

When the story was filed he was the chairman of the then-named Black Students' Union at the University of Toronto and the co-chairman of the conference. His photo and name, Selwyn Henry, appear alongside those of Amari Baraka, Louis Farrakhan, Burnley "Rocky" Jones—all noted political activists of the American and Canadian Civil Rights era and speakers at the event.

"What were you reading?" I ask, pointing at his image in the clipping.

"My speech," he replies.

"You gave a speech? What did you say?" I perk up with a sense of pride, although I'm uncertain what exactly there is to be proud about.

"Well, it wasn't really a speech. They were more like remarks. I probably said something generic about our attempt to build a unified international Black movement."

"There's nothing generic about that," I say, shaking my head.

The conference took place three years after the assassination of Martin Luther King Jr. and two years after the student-led uprising against racism at Sir George Williams University in Montreal. With the death of Dr. King and the call for "Black Power" reverberating up north from the United States of America, the actions of the students reflected the tenor of the times. Many of the students who were Black and from the Caribbean had left homes where the concept of a minority status was foreign. In fact, the Montreal Congress of Black Writers held in Montreal in October 1968 was seen as a watershed moment for many of Canada's Black university students. There, over four days, their sense of Blackness was lit on fire by Stokely Carmichael, Rosie Douglas, Miriam Makeba, C.L.R. James, and others.

"I saw Stokely in Montreal, somewhere in the crowd," my father says. "We didn't speak, just sort of embraced each other's fists over the heads that passed between us."

Stokely Carmichael embodied the 'nation within a nation' philosophy when he changed his name to Kwame Ture a year later.

"Really? Wow, that must have been surreal," I say, remembering the pictures I had seen of Stokely's fist held high when I started googling his name a few years back.

"It was, in a sense. I hadn't seen him since he left Oxford Street," he replied.

It wasn't until I was in my late twenties that I found out my father and Stokely Carmichael were born a year apart and lived across the street from each other on Oxford Street in Belmont, Trinidad. One day my grandmother sent me to get new bed linens out of her bedroom closet. I stumbled upon two large boxes filled with books. They were copies of *Ready for Revolution: The Life and Struggles of Stokely Carmichael (Kwame Ture)*. They were dusty but untouched by bookworms or termites. The Carmichaels, many of whom had migrated or were deceased by that time, had entrusted my grandmother with those copies for the community.

Twenty pages of the autobiography are dedicated to the first eleven years of Stokely's life in Belmont, the effects of the Second World War on his twin-island state's nationhood, and the country's eventual changing political and cultural grounding as an English colony.

Although he is not mentioned by name, my father lived among those pages. In fact, it's almost as though he could have written them with his own nuances of life in Freetown, so named for the former enslaved Africans who made Belmont their home a century before Stokely and Dad.

The year I turned twenty-nine, a commemorative plaque was erected on the wall outside the Carmichael's house by the Emancipation Support Committee of Trinidad and Tobago. As a designated heritage site, the house was to become a centre for learning. Young people from the neighbourhood would have access to a library and computers, as well as health and wellness workshops. However, the intentions of those well-meaning committees never materialized. Those books never made it from my grandmother's closet to those library shelves.

Selwyn was twenty-nine at the time of the 1971 conference in Toronto. He was also the father of three of my half-siblings. He left his two sons and his daughter with their respective mothers in London, England. He joined more than sixty thousand Caribbean immigrants who moved to Canada in the late sixties and early seventies, thanks to the Liberal government's reformed immigration policy. He was a student, held a part-time job at Toronto Western Hospital as a lab technician, and tutored Black youth through the Transitional Year Program at the University of Toronto. His work with the program and the Black Student's Union came in handy when he helped design what became known as the Black Education Project (BEP) alongside Horace Campbell.

"Do you think you changed anything? With the kids, I mean...did things get better for them?"

"Well, I certainly think so. We helped more Black kids access a university education for one," he starts. "With the BEP, well, even though the situation was not as bad as in the States or even as I experienced in London, Canada was not prepared for us. They didn't know how to deal with our language or our culture. You just had to look at what was happening in the elementary and high schools to know that. We were students ourselves and figured we could have an impact on Black kids."

Paradoxical is the word I think I'm looking for when he tells me about his community work and activism to benefit children. I think about my half-brothers and sister, at the time too young to go to university, but old enough to know that their father was absent. I think about the four of us who came later, after the young men and women Dad mentored were long graduated. How would our lives have been different if he was there to do our homework with us or tuck us in at night?

In the background, he continues to tell me about the struggles faced by Caribbean immigrant parents and the dangers of the subtleties of Canadian racism. But what I want to know is how he felt as a father during those times? It's the question I don't have the heart to ask tonight.

GLASS **LASAGNA**

— *C A S O N   S H A R P E* —

Ashley says the year after she finished school she blew her life up. We are smoking a joint outside of Concordia after hearing Lisa Robertson do a reading. I have been out of school for a year now and the idea of blowing up my life sounds appealing. I want to keep the good in and kick the bad out. Lisa Robertson is a chill poet, nothing bad to say. I don't always understand what she's talking about but she does her thing and I respect that.

Winter is almost here—I have to wear one of my heavier fall jackets outside or else I get sick. It's been raining for three days straight. I have to work tomorrow. I hate my job so much, but I don't know what else to do. I used to want to go to grad school but now I'm like, *No thank you*. I don't mean to be anti-intellectual about it; it's just not for me. Not right now at least. Take Lisa Robertson, right? I think I would've felt more defensive about 'not really getting it' had I still been a student, but since there wasn't going to be a test or anything I didn't really care. I liked the parts that I understood and that's fine. I'm sick of trying to prove to people that I'm smart.

It's Thanksgiving this weekend. Usually I go back to Toronto for Thanksgiving, but I didn't get it together this year. I've stayed in Montreal for Thanksgiving two times since I moved here five years ago, and both times friends have thrown elaborate dinner parties: wine flowing, a full turkey, and two dozen guests seated on either side of a long wooden table.

Kalale says Mada wants to do something more low-key this time around, just a few of us. No one's getting it together this year.

Later I go to karaoke at P'tite Place with some friends. I sing "A Simple Kind of Life" by No Doubt, which is not a crowd pleaser, but I have to—it's my favourite song. *And all I ever wanted was the simple things...A simple kind of life....*On stage I'm really feeling it even though nobody's paying too much attention. I really do just want the simple things, a simple kind of life, but recently everything feels so complicated: there is anxiety about the rent, my job that I hate, artistic ambitions left unfulfilled. When I finish the song Kalale does one of those finger whistles, which is impressive to me because I don't know how.

When I was a kid I affectionately referred to my generalized anxiety as my "worrywart disease." I chewed the collars of my shirts and cried whenever I was away from home for more than a couple of hours. I used to draw these portraits of myself as a teenager with thick Crayola markers. In these pictures, I rode a skateboard and wore a backwards baseball cap with baggy jeans. "Me at 16," I wrote at the bottom in crooked block letters.

Whenever I think about the future I think about these drawings, me riding down an endless suburban street on a skateboard, baggy pants, chain dangling from a belt loop, sun shining.

When I was about eight years old my teacher pulled me out of class one day and told me I was going to take a special test. I went into a little room next to the computer lab where you usually only went when you were in trouble, but my teacher made it clear that I was not in trouble. In the room there was a woman I didn't recognize. She wasn't a teacher or lunch supervisor or parent volunteer. I assume we introduced ourselves, but I don't remember. The woman asked me a bunch of different questions. She asked me to name five reasons why paperback books were better than hardcover. She asked me to arrange a series of flashcards in chronological order: a house at sunrise, a house during the day, a house at sunset, and finally, a house in the night. I sat with the woman for about an hour, just her and me, and then she sent me back to class. A few weeks later, my teacher had a meeting with my parents and told me I was gifted.

It didn't really mean anything to me. All it meant was that I got extra work if I finished a lesson plan early. There was another kid in my class who had been tested and who was also gifted. We were friends and would do our extra work together, sitting separately from the rest of the class. I'm sure we had little egos about it.

———————

I wake up really early the morning after Lisa Robertson/karaoke with a hangover and a plan to declare bankruptcy so I can get out of credit-card debt. I have so much credit-card debt, and suddenly it seems very important that it all goes away right now. Bad out. I have been putting it off and off and off. A collection agency calls me now. I have a mini half-conscious panic attack in my bed that eventually leads to clarity. I'm going to declare bankruptcy, I decide. I don't have any assets anyway. I don't know how to drive, and owning a home feels like it's out of the question. I open up my laptop, which sleeps next to me in bed like a surrogate boyfriend, and do the research.

Bankruptcy is wiped clean off your record in six years. I get out of bed and look out my window to the bakery across the street, the bakers setting up shop for the morning rush. It is still raining. The leaves on the trees are all yellow. In six years I will be thirty.

I take a shower and the whole time I'm like, *Bankruptcy, bankruptcy.* I call Zoe to tell her the plan. She says I should be more strategic about it. She says, "I want to move back to Montreal." I say, "I want to blow my life up and maybe move back to Toronto! Wanna swap?" She says, "Ha ha, yes, but where to work, and for you, where to live?" I hate that we live in different cities. I just want to watch TV on the couch with her like we did when we were kids.

Zoe is four years older than me, but we're also twins. I send her money when she needs it and she sends me money when I need it, no questions asked. I feel certain that one day we're going to be rich and famous, or at least professionally successful and materially comfortable. I tell Zoe that I hate my job. She says, "Me too." She says she thinks the baby she's nannying may be a secret evil supergenius. The baby is also teething and keeps trying to bite her. "Have you talked to Mom recently?" she asks. I haven't. "I have to go do work but I'm so hungover", I say. "Poor bunny," she says. "Yeah, I have to go deal with this crazy evil baby. Call me later this week; let's strategize."

I go to Cafellini to do work. I used to work in an office, but then one day my boss was like, "We're turning your office into a conference room," so now I work from home, which means from this cafe called Cafellini just outside Beaubien metro. The space is small with an awkward seating arrangement and only three outlets in the most inconvenient spots. When I started coming to Cafellini regularly the barista handed me a one of those punch-hole buy-ten-get-one-free cards.

She said, "You come here often," as if she were surprised to have a repeat customer.

All the baristas seem like best buds. They hang behind the bar, laughing and chatting during shift changes. They're all Francophone, white. They're always smiling. One of them makes a silly joke and they all groan. I imagine their lives are like a sitcom, the Quebecois version of *Friends*. They probably go out drinking together, just really living it up, you know? I am jealous. Working by myself can get lonely.

I work as a content writer for a digital marketing company. I write blog content for small businesses to increase their SEO, so they'll show up in Google searches more frequently. The trick is to embed keywords, or commonly searched terms, into the blog content to boost web traffic—so for instance, if I'm writing content for a plumbing business, I'll use terms associated with plumbing: pipe, valve, burst, faucet, sink. I mostly write for plumbing businesses, as well as a few contractors, a registered massage therapist and a German shepherd breeder, about whom I feel morally ambivalent. Every day I write between 1,500 and 3,000 words (depending on how productive I am that day) about plumbing, roofing, the benefits of massage, or German shepherd grooming tips. I get paid fifteen bucks for every article I write. My boss is always so impressed by the calibre of my work, which is frustrating. I have a BA and it's not rocket science—why wouldn't I be good at it? It's not very stimulating as work, but a job is a job. I wish I could work at a hip coffee shop like Cafellini, but my French isn't good enough. At least I'm not at the call centre anymore. Zoe says I have a unicorn job, because finding reasonable work with limited French in Montreal is basically a myth. Mom says my job is very millennial. When her dad was my age he worked in a factory; now I work at my computer.

————

Later that afternoon it is still raining and I am still at Cafellini doing work, kind of, when my roommate texts me to ask for our landlord's number. My mind immediately goes to bedbugs. "Is it bed bugs???" I text back. "No," she texts, "I need a letter for my student loan application." I send her our landlord's number.

I am always so worried about bed bugs, ever since that stupid sublet I had a few years ago brought them after he went to the Sochi Olympics. That sublet was the absolute worst. He moved into our apartment for six months and totally took over. He watched hockey on the TV in the living room every night and left dirty pots stinking of mac and cheese to stew in the sink for days at a time. My other roommate and I dubbed the sublet a Trustafarian, a rich white kid who moves to Montreal in order to 'slum it.' How could he afford to go to Russia to see the Olympics when he worked at a call centre for minimum wage? You have to watch out for people like that in Montreal, the white kids from Calgary or Vancouver who wear ripped jeans and always talk about how broke they are even though they go to Europe twice a year and never seem to have jobs.

One time I got high and watched the first season of *The Simple Life* with the annoying Trustafarian sublet. He was like, "Paris Hilton is so stupid," and then I had to explain the cultural significance of *The Simple Life* to him. In the first season of *The Simple Life*, Paris and Nicole spend six weeks living on a farm with a working-class family in rural Arkansas.

Paris and Nicole are positioned as these rich bimbos while their hosts are positioned as the pastoral ideal of hard-working moral purity. Running parallel to this portrayal is a second one that positions Paris and Nicole as enlightened cosmopolitans compared to the cultural ignorance and naivety of their rural foils. The competing frames create the central conflict of the show: working too hard leaves little room for one's aesthetic and cultural development, while having unlimited access to everything you want without having to work for it can erodes one's moral centre. The show is basically about capitalism. If I could quit my job tomorrow to do whatever it is that I wanted, what exactly would I do? Is work a moral imperative? I told my Trustafarian roommate, "That's what *The Simple Life* is about, man." After I finished my explanation, he was like, "Wow, you're really smart." Part of the reason I don't want to go to grad school is because I don't want to go further into debt to have people act all shocked when I say something intelligent.

Anyway, our Trustafarian sublet brought back Russian bed bugs from the Sochi Olympics. We cleaned our apartment and ran all our clothes through the dryer a bunch of times and had the place fumigated and then we were fine, but I'm still on edge about getting them again. There are no bed bugs in my apartment right now, thank god. The rain still hasn't let up. I only wrote a single article today: The Benefits of Installing a Backwater Valve. I am no Lisa Robertson, writing poetry for the cultural elite. The barista at Cafellini tells me that they're closing for the day. I write my boss an invoice for fifteen dollars. I finish the rest of my Americano, which has gone cold.

———————

Some days I feel unmotivated to write. I don't finish a single article, and because I get paid by the article, I don't make any money. Sometimes I work over the weekend, to make up for lost time. I don't watch movies or TV anymore. I'm too exhausted after work to do much of anything. Some days I think, *What's the point?* Nobody actually reads the articles I write. The articles are written to be read by the algorithms that scan the content for keywords so they can arrange Google results when someone searches a particular keyword. Basically, I write for an audience of complicated, highly intelligent software programs.

If a robot could write these articles, they would hire the robot. That's how everyone lost their factory jobs. Robots. I know that I am expendable, even though my boss is often "surprised" by the quality of my writing. I want to quit my job without giving any notice. I want to blow my life up and just walk away. I want to declare bankruptcy because it feels like a bottom to hit, from which I could rebuild.

On the way home from Cafellini, I call my mom and ask her what she was doing with her life at twenty-four. She says she was travelling with her boyfriend at the time, living out of the back of a van. How romantic. My sisters and I are the first in our family to go to and graduate from university. Mom says Zoe and I have access to futures she and Dad couldn't even fathom as possibilities at our age. I counter with this hypothetical: which is worse, to see no future at all or to see a future that is constantly just out of reach? Mom and I often come to these stalemates; I think it's a generational thing. Mom is sad I'm not coming home for Thanksgiving. I am sad too, but also relieved. I won't have to answer any questions about my job, where I'm headed in the future, etc. With sadness on one end of the spectrum and relief on the other, I am left in stasis, unsure what to feel. I tell Mom that I love her and end the call.

That other little gifted kid, the one with whom I did my extra work in elementary school, she lives in California now. She's a bioengineer. I don't know her salary, but I'm sure it's impressive. She's white. Her family is middle class, supportive. We see each other maybe once a year, when we're both back in Toronto for the holidays. Otherwise, she only exists to me via social media—hiking up a mountain in the Bay Area, giving a lecture at a women-in-tech conference. I like her and still consider her a friend, but I'd be lying if I said I wasn't jealous.

I think about the "Me at 16" drawings. What would a "Me at 30" drawing look like? I only wrote a single article today (fifteen dollars), two yesterday (thirty dollars), and four the day before that (sixty dollars). I feel out of options. Rent is due soon and I don't have enough.

———————

Later I go over to Mada and Kaeten's apartment on St. Andre for our low-key Thanksgiving dinner. It's still raining out. I wear a long trench coat and bring an umbrella. I arrive first with a salad. Mada and Kaeten make a lasagna, but the bottom element in their oven doesn't work so they're having trouble cooking it evenly. Mada takes the dish out of the oven and places it on top of a burning element. "That should cook the bottom, right?" she asks. Kaeten and I are like, "Yeah, sure." After a few minutes, Mada moves the glass lasagna dish to one of the unlit elements to cool down. There is a moment of silence and then the glass lasagna dish explodes into a thousand little pieces with a bang. It literally blows itself up. Bits of glass go all over the kitchen and into the living room. We sweep up the glass and throw it away.

"What should we do about the lasagna?" asks Mada. Kaeten thinks we can salvage it, but Mada is not so sure. Together they rescue what they can and put it onto a new pan that they place in the oven. Ella and Kalale arrive and we tell them about what happened. They laugh. "Don't you know that putting a glass dish directly onto heat is a bad idea?" Sometimes you just have to improvise, and sometimes that improvising doesn't go the way you want it to, so you have to improvise a solution. We decide to eat the lasagna anyway. Who cares? We start eating. No one bites into any glass. The lasagna is delicious. Outside, the rain has finally cleared. Kalale says she had a lot of fun at karaoke the other night, and I agree.

So what if I'm not in grad school? So what if I'm getting paid a measly wage to write blog articles no one will read? I'm not an engineer in California. I don't know how I'm going to pay rent this month. Everything is a big deal until it's not. I'll figure it out. I have to trust that eventually my life will come together and then probably fall apart again in some new way. At least I don't have bed bugs anymore. Of course, swallowing glass is always a possibility, but I have to trust that I won't.

HUNGER **GAMES**

A QUIZ

— *ROWAN MCCANDLESS* —

1. If you feed a fever and starve a cold, what should you have done about your eating disorder?
   a. You had no idea you even had an eating disorder. It always seemed a part of you, like a parasitic twin syphoning your self-esteem.
   b. You had some idea but were terrified to commit to change.
   c. Nothing. After all, you were told Black girls don't get eating disorders.
   d. Reach out for help because Black girls do get eating disorders, and there was no way you could overcome it on your own.
   e. Is this a trick question?
   f. You didn't want to believe that you even had an eating disorder. You were just extremely disciplined, had an abundance of food intolerances, a profound and abiding compassion for all living things except, perhaps, for yourself.
   g. Who are you trying to kid?
   h. All of the above.

2. Growing up, when people said, "You have such a pretty face," it wasn't meant as a compliment.
    _____ True   _____ False

3. You couldn't fight Mother Nature; big bones ran in your family.
    _____ True   _____ False

4. Check all that apply. Having an eating disorder gave you a semblance of:
    _____ Control when life was complete chaos.
    _____ Power to compensate for being powerless as a child.
    _____ Safety in a world that did not feel safe.
    _____ Mastery over your body; you could bend it to your will, whip it into shape, force your flesh into a package considered more palatable.
    _____ Self-esteem and validation within your family and society at large.

5. When you finally summoned the courage to walk through the doors of the Eating Disorders Program, which best represented your thoughts?
    a. Turn and run. Run, run as fast as you can. Things weren't as bad as they seemed, as you calculated how many calories you'd burn by bolting out the building to your car.
    b. You rationalized that there were far worse ways to abuse your body than having an eating disorder.
    c. Things were as bad as they seemed. So even if you had to force yourself, you were going to participate in the program.
    d. You should have arrived earlier and saved yourself the embarrassment of walking, in full view, in front of everyone seated in a semi-circle.
    e. Why didn't you try to lose more weight before entering the program?

f.   One of these things was not like the other—you were the only woman of colour in the group.

g.   You thought of a million other places you'd rather be.

h.   Forget those million different places. You needed this group, this program to get well.

i.   You were afraid that you didn't belong in the program. Then what would you do?

j.   You were afraid that you did belong in the program. Then what would you do?

k.   You were terrified that making peace with food and with your body would lead to massive weight gain.

l.   So obsessed with surface and appearance, your family wouldn't accept you if you gained weight.

m.   So obsessed with surface and appearance, society wouldn't accept you if you gained weight, and you already had one big black check mark against you.

n.   You couldn't imagine life without an eating disorder.

o.   All of the above.

6.   When you looked in a mirror, your image was often distorted, as if you were standing in front of a not-so-funhouse mirror at the carnival.

_____ True   _____ False

7.   The bathroom scale weighed and measured your worth.

_____ True   _____ False

8.   Fat is not a feeling.

_____ True   _____ False

9.   Giving up your eating disorder felt like you'd be:

a.   Abandoning your best friend.

b.   Ridding yourself of your worst enemy.

c.   Both (a) and (b).

10. You found the program and your counsellor to be:
    a. Supportive.
    b. Helpful.
    c. Guided by a feminist perspective.
    d. Empowering.
    e. Safe.
    f. All of the above.

11. Check all that apply. Have you ever wondered why your mother:
    _____ Never ate a meal with the family at the dining-room table?
    _____ Seemed to live on cucumber and cottage cheese?
    _____ Refused to have her picture taken?
    _____ Stayed with your father despite all his affairs?
    _____ Blamed you for ruining her life?
    _____ Put you on one fad diet after another, telling you children were starving in Biafra, China, down the street, so you had better clean off your plate?
    _____ Said repeatedly, "The world will screw you, just as soon as look at you"?
    _____ Doled out diet pills like communion wafers, teaching you that hunger was a sin and absolution could only be found in self-denial and starvation diets, long before you entered junior high school?

12. It was easier to count calories than the number of times your mother said, "You don't want to wind up some fat slob with your nose stuck in a book."
    _____ True   _____ False

13. Being "Daddy's little girl" was a privilege that came with a price.
    _____ True   _____ False

14. Throughout your childhood:
    a. Your father kept a gym bag filled with *Playboy* and *Penthouse* magazines and taught you that women were expected to look a certain way.
    b. You watched your father flirt with pretty women with peaches and cream complexions and tiny waists at the cosmetics counter at Eaton's Department Store.
    c. Your father had affairs. You know this because your mother treated you as a confidant; her shoulder to lean on; her cross to bear, because if it were not for you, they wouldn't have had to marry in the first place.
    d. All of the above.

15. One evening, a woman across from you in Group said, "Women of colour have it so much easier. They're okay with their bodies—with having bigger bodies. They don't have the same pressure to look a certain way—to be thin. It's harder for white women, all this pressure to be thin." Which best describes your response?
    a. You couldn't believe the words that had fallen out of her mouth.
    b. You pretended not to hear, not to feel the sting of her remarks.
    c. You avoided eye contact; watched the clock tick away until it was break time and you could escape.
    d. You counted snack-box raisins as if they were rosary beads and silently catalogued your faults; your body's numerous imperfections.
    e. You sucked in your stomach, tried to erase the trace of Africa from your big gal thighs by squeezing them together, prevent your flesh from spilling over the sides of the chair.
    f. You looked at her and wished you were that thin.
    g. You thought she didn't have a damn clue.
    h. You felt like a failure, a fraud, an outsider; apparently a restrictive eating disorder was not one size fits all.

i.   You wanted to say something but didn't want to be mistaken as the spokesperson for all women of colour.

j.   You didn't want to become someone's teachable moment.

k.   You didn't want to become a target by speaking up, be perceived as a rabble-rouser, the embodiment of the angry Black woman stereotype.

l.   You felt like a disappointment; that on behalf of women of colour, experiencing an eating disorder or not, you should have said something.

m.   You wondered how a statement of erasure and privilege could have gone unchallenged by the rest of the group.

n.   You thought: What must it be like to speak from that level of privilege? To simultaneously presume that she could speak for all women of colour—discounting the historical traumas inflicted on Black women's bodies since the slave trade—while she garnered sympathy for herself.

o.   You wondered: Why is the pain of women of colour so easily dismissed and ignored?

p.   You went completely still, desperate to fade into the background. You wanted to disappear—which, given your prior history and the nature of your eating disorder, seemed rather ironic.

q.   You swore you were done with the program; that it was no longer a safe space.

r.   All of the above.

16.   Growing up, playing the tent game with your father had nothing to do with the circus.

_____ True   _____ False

17.   Growing up, you were "Daddy's *little* girl," and your mother worked hard to keep you looking that way.

_____ True   _____ False

18. You cursed the sadist who designed your junior high gym uniform—the infamous Greenie—the one-piece, bloomer-bottomed bane of your middle school existence that exaggerated your round ass, burgeoning breasts, and child-bearing hips. On a scale of zero to ten, with zero representing no pain, and ten representing the worst pain imaginable, please quantify the awkwardness and discomfort experienced during your participation in gym class.

    no
    pain 0 1 2 3 4 5 6 7 8 9 10 worst pain
                                               imaginable

19. Check all that apply.

    _____ At twenty-three you were expecting your second baby. You met your father for lunch to share the exciting news. After you told him, he suggested that you have an abortion. He said, "You don't want to wind up some fat slob pumping out babies on welfare."

    _____ The day after you had your C-section, your father came to visit you in the hospital. The first words out of his mouth were, "Now what? I know a woman who was back at the gym a couple of days after having her caesarean."

20. At twenty-four, your mother looked at you in disgust and said, "You've lost so much weight that your arms are all flabby." You responded by:
    a. Thanking her for the concern.
    b. Joining a gym and working out two hours every day—on top of going to university, raising two small children, and working part-time.
    c. Smiling at her from across the dining room as you pushed food around on your plate, feeling this rush of power because no one could force you, no one could make you eat.
    d. Some of the above.

21. Why did you wage war on your body?
    a. You're not sure. This is what you were trying to figure out.
    b. Your body was under constant critique and criticism by your family. Appearance mattered above all else. Being the product of a mixed-race marriage at a time when that was unheard of, you were expected to bolster the family's image. Good enough wasn't good enough. A perfect family required perfect children.
    c. You were taught to fear fat like a frightened child feared monsters under the bed.
    d. Before 1963's March on Washington and Martin Luther King's "I Have A Dream" speech, your parents took you to have your portrait done. You sat on a stage, while the artist captured your image in oil pastels. Women in cotton dresses, high-heel shoes, bouffant hair tamed by hairspray, commented on your appearance, your stellar "children should be seen and not heard" performance as they stood next to men wearing summer suits and neckties, crew cuts covered by fedoras. You sat there afraid and in silence; body and character up for critique by strangers, while your parents stood off to the side, basking in the warm reception. It was on this day, shortly after your fifth birthday, when you realized how it felt to be an object.
    e. Throughout childhood, you spent your entire allowance on comic books and junk food. While your parents held screaming matches at home, you held story time and tea parties in the attic with your younger brothers. You sought solace in cans of rice pudding, Old Dutch potato chips, and Grimm's fairy tales.
    f. You saw no reflection of you or your family in your childhood reader, only sandy-haired twins, John and Janet, and their blonde-haired, blue-eyed baby sister, Anne. You didn't see yourself reflected in Miss Roma's Magic Mirror on *Romper Room*. Pudgy Black girls were not fairy-tale princesses.

g. As a child, Saturday morning cartoons characterized women of colour as either thick-waisted, thick-headed 'mammies' or hot-blooded, lustful 'Jezebels'—stereotypes meant to inspire shame. In print media and television, Black women played the role of happy domestics for white middle-class families. Our bodies were either bloated, corpulent caricatures used to sell everything from rice and pancake syrup, to kitchen memo pads and laundry detergent, or presented as half-naked, sex-starved and subservient 'jungle bunnies' for the benefit of the male gaze.

h. Systemic marginalization and erasure are exhausting. Maybe you thought if you can't beat them, join them. Make yourself literally disappear.

i. During Sunday dinners, your grandmother spoke of life in Nova Scotia. Between idle pleasantries and "pass the potatoes," she talked about Truro, how it was far worse than any place in the Deep South. She said, "People like to think that it's bad only in the States. But up here it's just as prejudiced. Worse." She spoke of race riots and segregation, as we piled our plates high with second helpings and sides of injustice.

j. You lived what you learned.

22. Family day at the beach. While you built sandcastles, a woman strolled by in a bathing suit. Your father laughed and said, "Just look at that beached whale."
_____ True   _____ False

23. Sticks and stones may break your bones, but names will never hurt you.
_____ True   _____ False

24. But names will never hurt you? Who came up with that phrase? You're confident whoever it was had never been on the receiving end of hate speech and called:
    a. Nigger
    b. Nigger-baby
    c. Watermelon bum
    d. Half-breed
    e. Mooolatto
    f. Slut
    g. All of the above.

25. Why did you try to make yourself invisible? Why did you want to disappear?
    a. Invisibility was safety. Unseen you couldn't be a target for racism.
    b. Invisibility was safety. Unseen you couldn't be mistaken for some hypersexualized, exotic other.
    c. Invisibility was safety. You learned early the vulnerability of Black and brown bodies. As a child, you witnessed unfiltered hatred on the playground, in the nightly news on television. The trauma of understanding that you were not safe in this world—simply because of pigment—is a fear that doesn't leave you. It became a burden that couldn't be shed, unlike weight.
    d. Invisibility was safety. No one could touch you if you were invisible.

26. Things you wished that woman from Group had understood before speaking out of turn and out of privilege:
    a. Your family worshipped the same impossible Eurocentric standard of beauty.
    b. The intersection between race and gender. Your body was under constant critique and criticism. The texture of your hair mattered. The pigment of your skin mattered. The size

and shape of your nose, your lips, your body mattered. You felt pressured by the weight of familial and societal expectations.

c. Eating disorders do not discriminate. For years you binged, starved, and purged.

d. Your family's fear that you would become "some fat slob" weighed heavier than any extra pounds you may have carried. They had swallowed the Kool-Aid without complaint; bought into "fat slob" as a reworking of the racial stereotype: Black women as "welfare queens," lazy and licentious, incapable of controlling their appetites, sexual or otherwise.

e. You were considered exotic, developed a body that men noticed whether you wanted them to or not.

27. Your first lover called you his Tahiti sweetie. He would go down on you while stroking your belly. He affectionately called it "your little anorexic stomach." He might as well have been saying, "I love you".

_____ True _____ False

28. You kept a photograph in your wallet. You were twenty-five; your eating disorder was completely out of control. In the picture your collarbone protrudes, your cheeks are hollow, eyes cloaked with sadness you were too blind to see. You called it your concentration camp photograph, and for some reason, to this day, you can't let it go.

_____ True _____ False

29. This is a long answer question. You may use additional paper, take as many breaks as necessary, in providing your response. How much did a history of sexual abuse in childhood contribute to your development of an eating disorder?

_____

_____

_____

_____

_____

_____

_____

_____

_____

_____

_____

_____

_____

_____

_____

_____

_____

30. After the incident in Group you decided to:
   a. Quit the program and never return.
   b. Take time to process what had happened; deal with your hurt, anger, fear, sadness. Group no longer felt like a safe space and you'd spent the majority of your life feeling unsafe in this world.
   c. Speak with your counsellor in the program and explain what those comments meant to you regarding personal experience, the myths surrounding women of colour and eating disorders.
   d. Address your feelings of being minimized, marginalized, erased.
   e. Speak with the woman who made the comments.
   f. Some of the above.

31. Circle all that apply. When your mother passed away, you inherited the portrait, the one of yourself at age five and fashioned in oil pastel. You are wearing a party dress—an impressionist pattern of soft teal, cream, and blue, with peephole cut-outs at the shoulders. Within that gilded frame, you are not smiling. The portrait hung in your parents' dining room for years, held you hostage to an ideal that did nothing but harm you. Once in your possession, you:

    a. Displayed the portrait in a place of prominence in your living room.

    b. Celebrated the feeling that you had rescued some essential part of yourself, that little girl who had no one to protect and care for her.

    c. Wrestled with the memories of vulnerability that the portrait raised.

    d. Struggled with disappointment—reclaiming the portrait didn't translate into the feel-good moment of triumph you'd long imagined.

    e. Hid the portrait at the back of your bedroom closet until you were able to accept the harm that was done to you in childhood.

    f. Talked about your grief in Group and with your counsellor.

    g. Reached out for help because Black girls do get eating disorders, and baby girl, you couldn't tame that beast on your own.

BECOMING A **SHARK**

REFLECTIONS ON BLACKNESS
IN CANADIAN WILDERNESS

— *Phillip Dwight Morgan* —

wilderness | ˈwildənis |
noun [usu. in sing]
an uncultivated, uninhabited, or inhospitable region

Little Black boys don't make compelling sharks, or at least that's what I thought growing up in Scarborough. We don't have gill slits or multiple rows of replacement teeth, and the proportions from our heads to our trunks to our tails are all wrong. I suspect that's why I failed 'Shark Level' in swimming lessons. It simply wasn't in the cards. Prior to that moment, I'd successfully convinced people that I was pollywog, tadpole, sunfish, and even dolphin. Becoming a shark, however, was far more difficult.

I recall standing on the white-tiled deck of the pool at L'Amoreaux Collegiate, shivering, as my wet blue and orange bathing trunks clung to my adolescent thighs like saran wrap and my matching blue goggles sat perched atop my head. Water dripped, then pooled, around my feet as I nervously awaited my report card from the swim instructor. As she handed it to me, my eyes zeroed in on two red Xs set apart from a column of green check marks. Apparently my whip kick was lopsided and I was eighteen seconds short of the two-minute treading requirement. Dejected, I slowly walked back to the changing room. If I wanted to continue swimming, I would have to repeat Shark Level.

Three months later, when I failed to become a shark for a second time, I decided once and for all to retire from swimming at the age of eleven and avoid pools whenever possible. Despite my best efforts, no amount of practice could secure my predatory acumen.

I hid from the pool at L'Amoreaux, located a mere two-minute walk from my house, and with each passing year its presence felt increasingly strange, even otherworldly; its acrid chlorine fumes serving as a constant reminder of the peculiarity of these places.

I desperately wanted to be a good swimmer but struggled with the coordination. I didn't see many other Black children at the pool and I recall feeling embarrassed when some of my classmates commented on my round tummy. In short, the pool was a space of alienation for me. In hindsight, I'm fairly confident that my fraught relationship with wilderness began here, in the pool, as an insecure Black boy.

As I grew older and saw other children exploring the outdoors with their families or attending overnight camps, I felt the all-too-familiar feelings of apprehension, fear, and alienation. I saw the uncertainty of the deep end of the pool mirrored in Canada's vast lakes and forests. The dense brush and thickets, much like the bodies of water they contained, could swallow children whole and steal them from their families, forever. The easiest and safest way to avoid this fate, I concluded, was to simply avoid such places.

It's not hard to see why I came to this conclusion. In addition to my own discomfort with water, there were larger societal forces at work—in film, television, literature, and visual art. Black people have been—and remain—curiously absent from the amalgam of snow-capped mountains, rivers, forests, and animals often labelled "nature" here in Canada. Similarly, Black people are rarely depicted in film, television, or books as adventurers, explorers, park rangers, or zoologists—people with a deep knowledge of their surrounding environment. Instead, we are passers-by, transients, vagrants—people who may be present in this vision of nature but clearly do not belong there. More often than not, we are depicted as gangsters and slaves, never managing to exist either comfortably or competently in nature. Our knowledge, much like the clothing we are shown wearing, is unapologetically urban and, therefore, alien to this particular vision of nature. There's a subtle but clear message here, the messaging of absence, working in tandem with these stereotypes to tell us that we are not only gangsters but gangsters unwelcome in Canadian wilderness.

Many Black folks have internalized this messaging. There are countless Black comedians who tell jokes about why Black people don't camp, swim, rock climb, or participate in outdoor activities. The punchlines oscillate between telling audiences that these activities are "white people things" or, less often but equally problematic, how evolutionary biology has taught Black people to fear these activities. In one joke about rock climbing, for example, a Black comedian riffs, "But why would Black people willingly participate in a sport where they have to put a rope around themselves?" The mostly Black audience quickly bursts into laughter.

There's a certain insidiousness to these narratives, a flexibility and dynamism to the process of othering that aches deep within my belly. On one hand, history shows us that Black folks have been labelled 'savages' and 'primitive' by colonizers to justify enslaving us and separating our bodies from the land. Our intense connection to the land formed the basis of a rationale justifying our oppression; it was a signpost of our 'otherness.' Now, in more recent years, Black folks have once again been severed from the land but, this time, it is because we supposedly do not possess the requisite knowledge for living on this particularly hostile and frigid land. According to this messaging, Black people simply do not belong in the so-called Great White North. This narrative has been reinforced time and time again in my life when, upon meeting someone for the first time, I am asked, "Where are you from?" followed by, "But where are you *really* from?" whenever the response "Scarborough" does not fit with their assumptions.

It was only when I left Scarborough at the age of seventeen that I began to examine my relationship with nature. At Trent University, I encountered a largely white and rural student population that, shockingly, laid claim to nature in ways that I'd never considered possible. Spouting stories of backcountry camping and the joys of the great outdoors, these students mobilized an entire wilderness vernacular that revolved around Thoreau, the Group of Seven, campfires, and portaging. As you can imagine, they were genuinely shocked to hear that I'd only been in a canoe once before during a grade six trip and that I had no knowledge of the Canadian landscape painter Lawren Harris.

In the shadow of their disbelief, I became intensely aware of the tremendous privilege and cultural capital often associated with accessing 'nature.' Despite all of the romantic musings about becoming one with nature, there is a material reality—the requisite equipment such as tents and sleeping bags—that is often prohibitive. It not only limits access to nature but, also, the much revered rest and relaxation that accompany outdoor recreation. How did you get to Rice Lake? How did you learn to paddle? Where did you get your skis or your winter ski pass? These conversations rarely occurred. Similarly, conversations about how camping and canoeing are often embedded within cultures can be unwelcoming, if not openly hostile, toward people of colour did not occur. As a young Black man from Scarborough studying history, the issue was not only that my family did not have a canoe or tent or ski poles or a cottage but, also, that we didn't feel like we had any basis for laying claim to those spaces. Perhaps on some level we, too, believed that our biology had estranged us from the land, carefully steering us from canoes to cul-de-sacs.

For these reasons and many others, I decided to make cycling across Canada a personal goal. At the time, I viewed a cross-Canada journey as a bold act of defiance, a way of legitimizing my relationship to a particular vision of nature, one with little room for the hydro fields, basketball courts, and shopping malls of my youth. Cycling across Canada epitomized ruggedness, adventure, and direct engagement with the elements. Secretly I hoped that perhaps, like Thoreau, I would experience great personal revelation during such a trip.

Although I had the audacity to imagine the trip, I was not so naive to think that I could do it alone. Cycling across Canada would require levels of confidence and skill so far outside of my knowledge and experience that to embark on such a trip alone would be reckless. The trip would also require a lot of equipment well beyond the means of a cash-strapped humanities student.

For years, whenever I met someone 'outdoorsy,' I dropped hints about my dream, secretly hoping that it would spark a curiosity in them as it had done for me. For nearly five years, everyone deemed the trip too expensive, too dangerous, or too difficult. With each passing year, the dream seemed increasingly unlikely. That was until Alex.

I still remember the day: Alex and I were running through Bayfront Park in Hamilton, training for a half-marathon. As part of our usual small talk, I mentioned that I'd had a dream of biking across Canada but that I'd been unable to find someone to do it with me. Without hesitation, Alex said, "I'll do it with you." I stopped running, looked at him, and asked, "Are you serious?" He replied as earnestly this time as he had before, "Yeah, when do you want to do it? April? May?" It was mid-February.

That weekend, Alex came to my apartment and began planning for a trip in May. Alex had done a few week-long trips. I, on the other hand, had never done any cycle touring. We generated an arm's-length list of gear to be purchased and tasks to complete. Among my top priorities was to secure a touring bike for the trip and to do at least a couple of 100-kilometre practice rides before we left for our trip.

As the trip approached, I began having intense visions of my own death, regularly tossing and turning in my sleep, routinely waking up in a sweat-soaked panic. After bumping into a friend who told me that he'd dreamt that I'd died on the trip, I became convinced that my nightmares were in fact premonitions.

Perhaps I was embarrassed by the number of people I'd told about the trip, too proud to cancel plans several years in the making, but, despite my fears of death, I still committed to going on the trip. As family members and friends questioned my decision, repeatedly asking whether I'd lost my mind, I quietly wrote notes to loved ones and stowed them in my desk in case I died.

After receiving a less than subtle nudge from Alex reminding me that I should do at least one practice ride before we departed in a week's time,

I biked forty kilometres outside of the city, stopped at a café for a crois-
sant and espresso, then turned around and biked back home. I arrived
back at the entrance to my apartment and I thought, "Well that wasn't
so bad," before starting on more important tasks on my list.

The first day of the trip, Vancouver to Whistler, consisted of nearly 120
kilometres of riding, most of it uphill, with a 700-metre elevation gain. I
thought I was comfortable riding hills; I wasn't. I thought I knew how to
shift gears; I didn't. I felt like a fool as my chain clickity-clacked its way up
the incline, occasionally dismounting the chain-ring to avoid further torture.
On several occasions, I stalled out on hills, losing all forward momentum
before slowly rolling backward and then falling off my bike. On those first
days, I seriously questioned my decision to go on this trip. In addition to
being a weak rider, I carried with me a profound fear of all the unknown
insects and animals lurking in the woods and mountains around me.

Several times per day I thought, "What on earth am I doing here?"

As time progressed, I became increasingly comfortable in the remote
parts of this country. One hundred and thirty-five kilometres of cycling
per day, six days per week, often in the absence of human contact, has
that kind of effect on a person. Three weeks into the trip, I knew that
something had seriously changed in me when I continued on my way,
seemingly unfazed, after nearly stepping on a large snake as I walked
through a wooded area.

Alex and I arrived in St. John's on July 5, 2012, 65 days and 7,706
kilometres after we began our journey. We spent the day receiving free
drinks from locals who were eager to hear stories of our cross-country
travel. After spending a few days in St. John's relaxing, we flew back to
Ontario. A week after my return, my family threw a party where I told a
captive audience of friends and family a well-rehearsed anecdote about
my run-in with a bull moose while cycling in New Brunswick. Mesmerized
and amazed by my tales, the guests spent the evening filling themselves
with burgers and corn on the cob and congratulating me on my accom-
plishment. There was a kindness and generosity of spirit present in all
of the guests that evening that I will never forget. For several months,
maybe even years after I returned, my mother's neighbour would greet

me with, "Man! I still can't believe you cycled across the entire country," whenever I returned home for a visit.

I am, truth be told, uninterested in recounting at length specifics of the trip. I've shared these stories dozens of times, each time making mental notes about where more flourish or a subtle pause will help pique interest. These well-rehearsed stories often rushed out of my mouth at parties and other gatherings, vaulting over tongue and teeth at the mention of the words "Canada," "bicycle," or "adventure."

In one sense, the trip couldn't have been more successful. Alex and I had achieved our lofty goal of cycling across the second-largest country in the world, and we each returned from the trip with a bursting catalogue of tales. I saw many landscapes and all number of flora and fauna; my connection with nature now went unchallenged by everyone around me.

In another sense, however, the constant retelling of these stories reveals a deep insecurity around my relationship to nature that has followed me from the pool to the mountains and back to Scarborough again. Every year, the fabled bull moose from New Brunswick has gotten closer and closer; the distance from here to "that lamp" shifting from twenty feet to ten and then five. For five years, I've remained stuck: stuck telling stories about bears, and snakes, and moose, stuck describing desert roads that lead to snow-capped mountains, stuck trying to fit those sixty-five days of cycling into a grand narrative about exploration and adventure where the chubby Scarborough boy in the bathing suit and goggles becomes a shark and finally belongs somewhere.

Perhaps this is simply the internal struggle for many Black children born in diaspora. Here, in this place we call home, the ways that our families engage with nature are rarely cherished or understood. My grandmother owns a farm and a popular restaurant in Jamaica. I've seen her slaughter a goat. Once, when I was about eight or nine years old visiting family in Jamaica, my grandfather trapped fireflies in a jar so that I could navigate a late-night walk. I was mesmerized by this tall silhouette of a man holding a jar of luminescence as we traversed the moonlight. My mother, who immigrated to Canada almost fifty years ago, can tell within a second whether a yellow yam is worth buying. There's a certain hue that my eyes have not yet learned to discern. For years, their experiences and knowledge were outside of my appreciation and understanding. Their ways of being did not fit my ideas of what it meant to engage nature.

It is only now, with the benefit of time and nearly 8,000 kilometres' worth of attempts to belong, that I am beginning to see the problems behind Canada's nature myth and the depth of humanity, experience, and richness it excludes. As time passes, the trip evolves and changes in my mind and the images of mountain passes, lakes, and fields are becoming increasingly hazy. Meanwhile, new insights are becoming ever clearer. My trip across the country was, at its core, a search for home, an ongoing quest for belonging in a country that is as much hostile and dangerous as it is rewarding. It was the sad effort of a chubby Black boy from Scarborough to become a mountain, a forest, an adventurer, and a grand narrative after failing to become a shark. It did not answer my deepest existential dilemmas but instead created endless questions. What is nature and what is wilderness? Why is our relationship with these concepts so fraught? How do we reconcile narratives of Black alienation from nature with the long history of Black settlement on this land dating back to the Black Loyalists? Why is nature so often depicted as either masculine or feminine, pristine or spoiled, white or Black?

Increasingly, I also wrestle with what it means to use storytelling as a way of laying claim to land that was stolen from the First Peoples. I see the futility of trying to assert belonging in a place so deeply invested in othering, a place where many thirst for ownership of land that never has been—and will never be—theirs to own.

With each passing year, I wonder how many more times I will tell friends and colleagues stories from my trip across Canada. How many more times will I feel these stories fighting to escape my mouth? Perhaps as many times as I continue to be asked, "But where are you really from?" whenever I say that I was born in Scarborough. Perhaps until the day when I learn to swim or finally recognize that unique yellow hue. Better yet, maybe this will be the last time.

HEAVY SCARVES

— *Fatuma Adar* —

'm in the stall, on the toilet seat, lifting my legs up against the door so no one recognizes my shoes. Girls from class enter the bathroom, clicking their kitty heels and laughing. I hold my breath, but they're too giddy and gabby to even notice I'm here. Giggles. Clicks. Swoosh. Silence.

They're gone.

I was terrified that my friends would come looking for me. I didn't have a language to explain what I was doing in there.

I press the pin from my scarf against my finger, but the stings aren't distracting me. I shift around nervously on the seat and fabric starts sliding off my head. My reflexes put it back in its place, starting at my hairline and wrapping it securely, but I'm still holding the pin in my hand.

In grade six I didn't know how to feel about my hijab. Sometimes it wrapped around me, cozy like a blanket, and other times it felt constraining, like a tight collar you had to stretch loose in order to breathe.

More girls come into the bathroom. Music from the hall comes flooding in and the sound tingles in my throat. I don't get to listen to music much. Although, I borrowed Harpreet's soundtrack to *The Lizzie McGuire Movie* and never gave it back. The DJ is playing Atomic Kitten and I'm surprised that it isn't enough to move me out of my seat.

My mom used to listen to music. She used to dance around with a gigantic shiny scarf, her garbasaar, in her hands and move her hips so quickly it made her laugh. She would wrap it around my waist, tell me to move like she did, but it was useless. "Dabo malaas," she'd laugh. "No ass." She seems happier now, but I catch her listening to old folk songs from time to time. A man would sing a cappella about narrowly escaping the wars that had passed, but my mother said it wasn't music, it was better termed as poetry. I quickly learned that it didn't count as sinful if it's part of your culture.

Giggles. Clicks. Swoosh. Silence. I think that I made the wrong choice. Students have the option of doing something else on 'Play Days'—the dance, movies, or study hall.

Muslim kids watched movies. But I refuse to sit through another screening of *Big Fat Liar*. I've got to go to the dance. My stomach lurches and I search my backpack for some snacks, sure that by the time I build up the courage to leave the stall there will only be pepperoni pizza left.

In a school filled with a bunch of Hindus and Muslims, cheese pizzas never stood a chance. I coerced my mother into giving me money for lunch that morning. I rarely asked, so she gave me five dollars for a poutine and gave my brother my tuna sandwich. It cost three dollars to go to the dance. This was also how I eventually paid Harpreet back for taking her CD.

I bring my feet down to the floor but they continue to shake. I manage to change out of my skirt and into a pair of jeans along with a silvery top my mom bought me for Eid. The silk felt electric on my skin.

There was always a rule. If I wore jeans, the shirt needed to be very baggy. Having the inconvenient occurrence of developing too quickly makes a mother throw boy's sweaters at you. The clothes did their job at concealing and were fantastic hand-me-downs for my five little brothers. If I wore a skirt, the shirt could be fitted. Positive reinforcement, I guess, to get me to stop wearing the baggy sweater and jeans option.

Most of the dance is over and I'm still in the bathroom stall, playing with the pin and readjusting my hijab. I start to think that the smell of the bathroom has already stained my clothes and if I leave now maybe I can catch the end of the movie.

I swore to myself for weeks that I wasn't going to wear it that day. I planned to slip it back on right before my dad picked me up in his cab, no one the wiser. A couple moments of bareheaded freedom, that was all I wanted.

My breathing becomes shallower and I roll my fingers into fists. Nerving myself up, I rip off the scarf dramatically, like a villain revealing their true form. But I don't cackle in triumph, instead I hold it crumpled in my hand and am immediately uncomfortable with the breeze blowing against my bare neck.

I'd worn the hijab since I was six, and as a kid I was occasionally teased. Nothing really creative, but most commonly I was asked if I was bald under my scarf. I was not. But in that moment I felt as bald as a mannequin, a sad plastic attempt to look human.

When I take my scarf off at home, it's safe, a relief. In the privacy of the stall no one sees my hair, but I feel naked. Even all alone it feels like someone is watching. I'm not sure what's left of me.

I'd released all my secrets. They floated out of my mind, through my hair and into space. I stared at the object in my hand with new eyes and saw it as something other than what people told me it was. Not as something that made me different from others and not as something that united me to some bigger picture. I looked at the delicate piece of cloth as it sat heavy in my hands and asked myself what it meant to me.

What are you?

I didn't want to be a crusader. I didn't want to be a victim. I just wanted to go to my grade six dance, without guilt, without the weight.

No one has phantom limb syndrome with a scarf, I tell myself. I'm just being a typical preteen, melodramatic about fitting in. Cry it out and move on. I fail at mustering up any tears, causing my face to twist.

My parents are both immigrants, who at my age had 'actual problems.' If I spoke to them, they'd make an attempt to understand, but they couldn't. If I spoke to friends, they would be so distracted by the 'barbaric' nature of our customs that they couldn't bring themselves to relate.

Parents couldn't understand. Friends couldn't relate. The thought sung in my head all throughout grade school. A melody that I felt only other first-generation Somali-Canadian Muslim girls could really hear. I was so many adjectives and so few verbs.

I walk out of the stall and toward the sinks. I force myself to look up into the mirror and I have a hard time processing what I see. I look thin, then round. Bottom half matryoshka doll, top half Betty Spaghetti. My silhouette against the backdrop of the cold, blue, metal stalls, instead of the warm, cream wall tiles in my home bathroom, looks unnatural. If I walk out that door people will think I've been starved just because they've never been introduced to my head sitting on my neck; they are only familiar with my face surrounded by the rippling clouds of my scarf.

I didn't look prettier with or without it. But people would continue to tell me one way or the other for the rest of my life.

The door swings open and I flinch, sure that for a slight second I've been exposed to all the school. Indian girls from another class walk in, smile, and don't say a thing to me. They continue to talk about the boys they like who refuse to dance. I eye their beautiful waist-long hair as I run a finger through my puffy and dry curls. I fooled myself into expecting a Rapunzel-like mane to cascade down as I pulled away my scarf, but instead my hair stood still in its place, unmoved by my decision to set it free. I've been duped, exchanged one burden for another.

I had never met my hair. I didn't know how it behaved in the wild. Would it bounce if I danced to the music? Would it fall in front of my face and block me from seeing what others were saying? During Ramadan a few years later, my mother lets me relax my hair. Chunks of it fell off within days. It was the first time I truly saw the hijab as a blessing.

The girls leave. I smooth out the scarf, hover it above my head, and set it down like a crown. I fasten the pin and let out a sigh doused in disappointment and relief.

I wasn't sure if I was taking a step forward or backward. I just knew in that moment that I was not my hijab, but I also was not the absence of my hijab.

I open the door and walk out into the dance to join my friends. Jeans, silver top, and scarf.

I couldn't say if I was happy with my choice, but I was thrilled to discover that I had one.

IN CHAYO'S **CAB**

AN INTERVIEW WITH
CHAYO MOSES NYWELLO

— Whitney French —

This is an edited conversation with Chayo Moses Nywello, a former cab driver based in Terrace, British Columbia. He was asked about his work and his experiences being a Sudanese immigrant and what it means to be a Black man in Canada.

Could you tell me a bit about your personal experience being a taxi cab driver?

It was bittersweet being a taxi cab driver, it's hard to tell if people are laughing or crying. Except the Irish: they are very clear, they are very black and white, very expressive. The same way they feel inside, you can see them express it. But I am existing in a culture that is grey. It is difficult to read the emotion. You just lean back and watch. Then you can learn and pick up. I was very humble to learn and I had to accept that I am a man with enough patience to understand. All the human race is born by Blacks; the whites didn't fall from sky, they were born by Blacks.

They need to stop fooling around.

I don't drive cab anymore. It was too much. I took on this job to get to know the community, the other part of community I did not know. I come across so many people as a taxi driver: doctors, scientists, drug dealers, different organized crime network, businessman, ordinary citizens.

Point to point. Through all this I got to know the multicultural make-up of this nation. I got to do all that I like to do. [Now I am] a driver by shuttle, all the Europeans who come for the skiing, all parts of the world, even Australians who come to ski. Business [people], wildlife photographers, frontier ski[er], I deal with many, many people; the only people I don't like are people those who are drunk.

So that's good.

Yes, please elaborate about the new position you have and how it is different than driving cab.

Because my [new] service [is] from airport to hotel or business place to business place, I book people for wedding, these are the people I deal with, mostly business classes. It is good; as a people person, I like to deal with them. I do expediting for WestJet and Air Canada; when customers lose luggage, the next day I deliver.

It is a good thing to be humble to different people. I respect who they are. I have to respect people and their opinion, but I still have the courage to tell the truth and say this is where I stand in life, especially in my personal life. That is their personal life; that is where they stand. I cannot shame them. I did not create you. Freedom of choice. I am humble to do all this work.

There is a negative and positive. They are reciprocal in relations or social interaction, but to be specific, it made me to think because what is funny to me may not be funny to you. Most of my experience as a taxi cab driver is trouble: drunk people who do not listen.

Do you have a story about people in your cab that you are willing to share?

One day I picked up a most wanted guy from Port Nelson who wanted to escape to the United States, to get an exit to Prince Rupert Port through Alaska. Based on what he told me, he had a Russian girlfriend that was a spy. Prime Minister Steven Harper was kicking out spies; "Do you think the Canadian government would book me and kill me for my Russian girlfriend?"

As a cab driver, you must be a person with patience.

I'm also an ex-military person and I worked for the UN, so I know some things. Former President Dick Cheney was in Smithers. How do you know all of this? Yes I know these things, because I am human being in the community.

I told him to pay me cash up front.

On the radio, they say we have a problem. "Yes, I know."

When you take on the job there is a conviction that you may be in danger. Like the soldier who says, "I am going to die," but it's their conviction. That I am of the National Defense, so it is their conviction that makes them go into death, they do not turn their back on it. So there's a liable of death in my job.

We left the liquor store. He wants to use the washroom. The RCMP they come, I look at him, I turn my head to the right to point that he is in the station, a silent communication. He took off, from the bathroom station. Husky.

So the RCMP went back into the car and took off. They communicated on the radio, they know where we were going, Prince Rupert. You see where I took you [Whitney] to Kitsumkalum, that saw mill there, that's where I saw the hitchhiker.

"Are you a good man? Can we pick up the hitchhiker?"

"I don't mind to pick him up, Chayo."

The hitchhiker downloaded the illegal music and sells them for like three dollars or five dollars, so we hit the road to Prince Rupert. Almost one hour and thirty minutes of driving. He asks, "Can I drink?" so all of them were having fun drinking a beer, shouting, shouting, everything coming out of his mouth. On the other side, the RCMP with three trucks were waiting for us. It was the RCMP from Terrace that told the RCMP in Prince Rupert, so before the road could branch off. Prince Rupert is a port, it's water. It's the end of Highway 16. So the RCMP is smart enough, they wait for us at the turn off. There was a chance that we could go to the Port Edward.

So we went there. The RCMP were waiting as soon as we arrived, everything turned off, what is called 'ghost car,' it is just a civilian car, on my other side was the two trucks. The truck on the right pulled from where it was from on the edge of the road, into the land to block me.

Yes, I said to myself, *we are coming to the end of the problem*. They turned around, they went behind me and we are blocked. RCMP truck on the right, front, back, and left; the only place to go is the water. The RCMP jumped out of the truck while it is still running. Right away I stop, park the car, they grab the guy and handcuff him. It was peaceful without blood or incident.

"Did he pay you?"

"Yes, before we left Terrace."

"Ok, good! Who's he?"

"A hitchhiker."

It was a funny story because there was no blood and no death. If it went wrong it could have been a chaotic problem. The same, life is life. When you go on the road, it is a part of the daily. Anything can happen. With the shuttle business, there's no bad experience. These are high business-class people.

Living in Terrace, BC, it is likely different than back home, but you mentioned that there are similarities as well?

What is relevant to where I was born and Terrace? It reminds me of countryside life, the farm where I was brought up. We milked the cows, then we take off and go to school in the morning, we come back in the afternoon, we go fishing to the river Nile side, around 5:30 a.m., we go diving in the water, swimming, we come follow the cows home. Use smoke to keep away the flies, we tie them down, dinner, we go to storytelling with Grandmother, the younger ones go to sleep, the older ones go to music until 11 p.m.

We go to fishing and go to hunting. On my Facebook, there's a lot of pictures of fishing and hunting, it's most enjoyable. And the nature, mountains, green, ocean. That is why I love it. It's both; you have city life too. Big city, it's stressful and full of traffic jams. You get on the road, your time is controlled by being behind the wheel, your heart is beating to get to the work on time, and then, the time you get home and dinner, you turn on the TV for a short time. City life with all this traffic and headache is no good for me. I had this experience in Egypt. It's no good. I would have to park by the roadside to catch the high-speed train, when I go to Vancouver or Calgary. I said no. Here I can drive, I am not worried about traffic or stress. I can go fishing.

I go to Skeena River, Kalum River, and the other small creeks. If it is a beautiful sunny day, I go to the ocean, waterfront near Prince Rupert. In front of the blue, blue water. If you don't want to be in the community, you can go to the bush, away from the pollution. There is a difference between dealing with people but also dealing with nature and the wildlife. I like to be in the bushes. It is good for me.

Do you wish to share a bit more about your upbringing?

I was born to a religious, conservative, agricultural family. These times I was brought up in, it was inclusive not exclusive. There's a nice switch, to liberalism. [It] is a bright idea. This system is excluded the more you have segregation. An in-group and an out-group. When the in-group gives you room, there's room for everybody, all the nations of the world, that's why I switched over [from conservative politics]. I found a lot of contradictions.

There are people in Canada who have the right to voice an opinion, and people who do not. It is deception and delusion. Those rights come from the Charter, from the United Nations. And it is a lie. Every day you see this hypocrisy. I have rights, free thinking, but Chayo...you should not have said all of this. My skin colour makes me an enemy. Push that under the carpet in the name of anti-war. I cannot go and talk about injustice of another if there is injustice here in my own home. But injustice has been used as a mechanism of survival for the particular group of people in power and at the same time they say there is injustice in another nation. I have to clean up my house before I go to clean up someone else's house—if they are ok for me to clean it. If not, it's their loss.

PhD holders are taxi drivers; a man who have no fear to speak the truth is true. New immigrants with bright ideas are true, but they do not want that contribution in Western civilization. They put them aside and hide the bright ideas. The good and the worst part of this country is going to be stalled. You remember we talk around this table, you can't see the problems because you were born from inside the cultural blanket and that blinds you. Something needs to be fixed.

You cannot pray for rain and don't want to deal with mud.

Can you, in as much detail you feel comfortable, share your first few weeks coming to Canada?

In June 2006, I arrived in Canada. I flew from Egypt to Frankfort Airport for four hours watching World Cup on TV, then I flew to Vancouver, then to Smithers. When I arrived, I was picked up at the area. It reminded me of some areas in Ethiopia. My sponsor picked me up and I went home. The weather, even on June 14th, it was too cold for me. I spent four days in that house and after that I got my own place in downtown Smithers. Two people—one for a honeymoon and one for wedding at the lumberyard—helped. I took over that job, but then I took over as a truck driver for a furniture place.

But at the Smithers lumber yard, all the time they see me, many times in a day, they kind of stopped, [to look at me looking] at the Hudson's Bay Mountain. She has been observing me stopping and looking up, I said, there was something I used to see on the TV in Africa, it is called snow.

"One day, it will come down here to this ground."

"Why does it come from the mountain, down to the ground," I asked.

"It is a natural process," she said. "In October or November the weather starts to get cold, the tree leaves turn yellow, and the weather gets colder and colder and colder, and in some areas the snow will come on the ground. There is something called frost and you will see it on the ground. You will see it coming down, down, down, until you see the snow on the ground."

I said "Good. But I want to see the snow up there on the mountain."

"We will take you there up one day on the weekend and touch it with your own hand."

"Yes, I'm ready for it."

So one day we went up the Hudson Bay Mountain, the road goes like this, zigzag, Feena and Inere, her husband is a radio technician. We are going to park the car and walk. Oh, ok, we go. We walk all the way. I could not wait to lay down and fall down like this. So it was in July, two week after arriving. Emery got the snowball when it is fresh and we throw it at each other. But it was cold up on the mountain. We spent a good time up there and now I am relaxed. I was anxious to see it. At last, I touched the snow. I sent pictures to Africa, sent this to Mommy. This is what we see. But I was waiting to see it on the ground.

It occupied my mind, this is what is going on in my head all the time. Around three in the morning, it was heavy, the weather felt heavy, then I [went inside the] house, to keep warm. I got up and looked through the window, I can see the snow and I went crazy. I was anxious to call back home, but I didn't want to wake them up. I sat at the window to look at the snow. We bought a shovel the other day.

"How do you like it, Moses?"

"I love it!"

"There is something we do here. It's called snow angel."

"Oh, ok."

Is there anything else you would wish to share for the interview?

Your title is accurate. People younger and older who are lost because their culture has been crushed and social order has been destroyed, this chaos, they become prey.

There is no social order to protect them, they look at themselves as inferior, even their life don't matter any more, we can go deep with this human psychology.

So now I'm going to put a little bit of conclusion on the topic. The reality is, you cannot destroy the race; you can try hard, but in the end it is a mutual destruction. This was tried in Egypt and Northern Libya.

We are witnessing the backfiring. To be reminded that our thoughts matter, our inventions matter. We do not believe that we are inferior. We believe in mutual respect. The moment you believe them is the moment your life doesn't matter to you. It is a world, in this universe, it doesn't matter what power they possess, human is human. We will say enough is enough.

Thank you for this title. He who decides to be an enemy to Blacks... good luck. It will catch up to you.

Blacks are productive.

UNINTERRUPTED

— *MÉSHAMA ROSE EYOB-AUSTIN* —

I have frequented a total of four schools during my ten years of education and I have yet to find an environment where race wasn't an issue. My first elementary school was where a classmate introduced me to racism. She found it amusing to tell me I looked like poop. I did not know how to deal with that so I told her she looked like a toilet bowl. It's a funny story to tell now, but the fact is I was dealing with a racist seven year old who knew she was doing something wrong but didn't know what and I already had an automatic self-defence mechanism in place to respond. By the age of seven I had been to more conferences than I could count, had attended numerous lectures, and had listened to countless conversations between my parents and their friends about race and racism, and still when it came to that moment where I found myself facing racism, I didn't know what to do.

Since then, most of my encounters with racism have been a little less obvious. In fact, they were only obvious to me because either I or a friend was experiencing them. An example of this would be my music class at school, where all the students with 'attitude' were given the same instrument to play and restricted to one tiny room while the rest of the class played together in the main room. Not surprisingly, all those students were kids of colour. In fact, the only students of colour in that main room were myself and a boy who, like me, only whispered about two words during class. Although most of the white kids in the main room with me didn't think about it in that way, they nevertheless had full access to the teacher who invested her time into nurturing their minds with the beauty of music, whereas she left those five children of colour to come to class feeling unwanted. It was also common practice to have at least one of the five kicked out of class during the short fifty-one-minute period. To know that I should consider myself privileged to be treated equally to my white peers and that this privilege could easily be taken away, was a burden. I often endured teasing from my friends, who would say I got preferential treatment because our teacher considered me to be the 'whitest' of the Black people in our class. I understood where they were coming from. After all, my teacher must've thought it was out of the ordinary to have a Black child whose parents were actively involved in her school life and maintained communication with her teachers, and I'm sure this was reflected in her behaviour towards me. This is not to say that Black children do not have present parents. Rather, white teachers treat Black students wrongly with the assumption that they have an absent or uninterested parent who does not take notice of their school life.

Less than a year ago, I had my first conversation about race in my school with my principal. Because of the lack of representation at our school, my friends and I had been talking about what it would be like to have a Black vice-principal. The word 'nigga' was used at some point. A teacher down the hall in her classroom overheard our conversation and came out to talk to us. Her main concern was not that we had used that word but that we had been talking about having a Black vice-principal. We told her we had nothing against our current VP and we were just reflecting, and her response was something like, "So? What difference would it make? You shouldn't be talking about him like that." My friends and I stood there in shock wondering what we had said to trigger such a reaction. Why did this white woman in a position of power feel threatened by these four Black girls having a profound and important conversation about race in their school? Had she really been listening, she would have known that we just wanted to feel a little less alone in this school where there were only six Black staff members to match the huge Black student population. This teacher was so 'disturbed' by our conversation that she reported it to our principal and my friend was suspended.

The reaction to this private conversation between friends had shown me the true colours of the staff at my school and it did not sit well with me. So with this incident in mind, and with the knowledge that my music teacher also treated children of colour strangely, I spoke up. I spoke with my parents and they both agreed that I should go speak to my principal not only because what happened was wrong but because it had a lasting psychological effect on me and my friends. We no longer felt we could speak freely between each other; we felt stripped of our right to privacy and felt silenced. We still had three years left at that school, and since we had no intention of leaving, we were determined to make some changes. I asked my mother to schedule an appointment with the principal and if she could be present during the meeting to support me morally and as a witness. I told all my friends this news and they were ecstatic! They could not wait for me to "put the principal in her place." I felt safer and stronger knowing that everyone had my back and was rooting for me. I walked into my principal's office nervous but sure of myself. I was not ready for the conversation that followed.

I did not expect my principal to be happy with a fourteen-year-old student coming in her office and telling her that there was a race problem at her school. I expected her to dismiss the idea—she did. She focused solely on the girl element of my story and dismissed the role of race in the incident. Her idea was to do a 'girl power' related workshop or assembly of some sort; all this so she didn't have to do anything about race matters. Her 'I don't see colour' response was so typically Canadian I almost laughed. Her refusal to acknowledge the role race played in this situation demonstrated to me just how much work needs to be put into the education system regarding race matters. By then I had completely shut down and was tearing up because I was frustrated with my inability to speak my thoughts. My body had gone into a kind of shock mode as a result of being dismissed in such an obvious way, and by then I was just nodding my head in agreement with everything she said so I could get out of her office. My mom was not letting that happen. My principal asked my mom if she had any suggestions, and she had plenty. My mother made her pay attention to what was taking place in the present moment.

My mother informed the principal that I wasn't listening to her, I had clammed up mentally and had removed myself from the situation. She told her that her refusal to acknowledge my Blackness was a refusal to acknowledge me because I was speaking to her of my experiences in relation to my Blackness. Blackness is an essential part of me and it is part of what shapes me. Had I not been Black, I would not have gone through all these experiences that have taught me to identify racism even when others don't think that's what it is. My mom then asked me if I had anything to say. I replied yes. I had a lot to say.

Uninterrupted, I detailed my experience as a Black girl in this school. I told my principal about the stereotypes the teachers had about Black students, the lack of patience and tolerance for us, and the feeling that we were expected to fail. As I spoke I felt my strength coming back, along with a sense of empowerment. When I stopped speaking I realized just how quiet the room had become.

I was born in Montreal to two immigrant parents: an Ethiopian mother and a Jamaican father. My parents were aware that my school environments would not nurture my need for Black role models so they made sure I was exposed to that outside of school. I was fortunate enough to have access to conferences, meetings, important figures, and books that helped shape my understanding of why and how Black is beautiful. However, they also understood the importance of recognizing the land we are on. My paternal ancestors were ripped away from their land, enslaved, and shipped off to the Caribbean. I do not know my origins, I can only make educated guesses. Every day I pray that my ancestors' land is being respected and their experiences are being valued and respected. With these thoughts in mind, it makes it very hard for me to be comfortable living on Indigenous land that was also ripped away from its first inhabitants. It is difficult to see the misrepresentation and lack of Indigenous perspectives when learning about Indigenous people. In my opinion, the racism experienced by Black folks is similar to the racism experienced by Indigenous people. Religion and violence have been used as systems of oppression against both groups. Through religion and violence our communities were taught to hate their cultures and were made to feel inferior. Women were devalued and treated with indifference instead of being respected for carrying our future. Racism in Canada has had a direct impact on Indigenous bodies and the cases of Missing and Murdered Indigenous Girls and Women is a prime example. This type of violence, which disproportionately affects Indigenous women, was unrecognized for decades simply because it was affecting them and not white women. A system was created specifically targeting the bodies and minds of Indigenous people, and a similar measure continues to be used to oppress Black people. A major difference between Blacks in Canada and its Indigenous population is that Indigenous people are still living on the land that was forcefully taken away from them.

I think that in order for any real change to happen in Canada, people need to acknowledge that racism exists here. Racism is an institutional problem; in order for it to disappear, the system in which we operate needs to change or disappear. There are many people who say that our system has failed us, but I disagree because it was never meant for us. Therefore, we cannot rebuild this system because that would mean tearing it down and completely rebuilding it from the start. If that is going to happen, then we may as well just create a new system. We need a system that recognizes that race is fictional. We need a system that will repair the damage done to minority groups and that creates an environment with equal opportunities so that Canada can truly be the land of the free.

PROGRESS **REPORT**

— *Christina Brobby* —

Dear Sir,

Almost forty years ago, I sat in your office with my (now ex) husband as you told us that our immigration application for Canada had been approved. We'd qualified based on points earned by finding my husband a job as an auto mechanic from the notice board at Canada House. I remember completing applications for him for jobs in places that I'd search for on my son's toy globe—Regina, Hay River, and finally, Grimsby, Ontario, which he accepted. I wonder what you thought of the Black couple sitting opposite you, she only twenty-one, and already parents to a preschooler? We were living in public housing and couldn't imagine owning our own home even though we both worked full-time. I wanted more from life, articulated by my vague complaints of a British class system that limited opportunities for young people unless they came from the right background. At the end of our meeting you shook our hands, wished us luck, and said, "If you get a chance, let us know how you're getting on. People do from time to time." So, here it is, my interim report on life in Canada, albeit rather late.

When we left London on a cool, cloudy, mid-summer day, it was my first experience on a plane; the furthest I'd ever traveled from England was on a high school day trip to Calais, France. I was exhausted from days of emotional farewells with the family and friends we were leaving behind and my young son's endless questions about our upcoming adventure that I couldn't answer.

In my corduroy pants and heavy wool sweater-coat, I was unprepared for the wall of heat and humidity that hit me when we emerged from Toronto's international airport. I knew about my new home; I'd envisioned a cold, dark, forbidding land and wasn't prepared for a place where you could wear open-toed sandals and sleeveless dresses for weeks without needing a cardigan.

We stayed for a while with friends of friends, an upwardly mobile Jamaican couple living in North York, who was the epitome of what hard work could get you in Canada. They each owned a car, were saving for a home, had well-paid jobs, and could afford trips back to England and Jamaica.

How naive we were! Grimsby was close to a three-hour return trip in heavy traffic from North York. For the first couple of weeks, Mike stayed in a motel during the week and returned home on the weekends. I visited him once, and left with impressions of long rows of cars parked outside boxy, low buildings beside a busy road. We never gave it a chance and made the arbitrary decision not to raise our son in small-town Ontario. Mike found work in Toronto, and I found temporary office jobs—typing up gold and silver certificates for those wealthy enough to invest in commodities. For the first few years, I spent a lot of time convincing my husband that we'd made the right decision and hoping that his threats to return to England were hollow (as an aside, Sir, I saw my ex-husband in Toronto a couple of years ago. He's still planning on returning to Britain).

In my legal secretarial course, I met a woman who changed my life when she offered me employment in the Bay Street law firm where she worked. My decision to become a legal secretary was, I confess, spurred by my interest in being paid as much as possible for the hours my fingers pounded a keyboard. Medico-legal, wills, estates, corporate, commercial, personal injury litigation: I worked in many areas before the naivety resurfaced—I saw no reason why I couldn't be sitting behind the desk in an office with a view of Lake Ontario instead of the cubicle I shared with another secretary.

My decision to go to law school reminds me now of my emigration experience—I was unprepared, but somehow it worked out. By then, Mike and I were separated and my son was in high school. The new man in my life, Clive, bore the brunt of my insecurities and fed me on weekends while I studied.

At the end of my second year as a law student, I gave in to my interest in northern Canada and found a summer job in Whitehorse, Yukon—by then I could easily locate it on a map. I worked for a lawyer who practiced criminal defense and family law. Between errands, I'd watch her in court, conducting a vigorous cross-examination of a Crown witness or delivering impassioned submissions to the judge. I knew then what kind of law I would practice.

I'm pleased to report that I survived law school. I went on to secure an articling position in Canada's largest criminal defense firm. Sir, the sad reality was that most of the firm's clients were young Black men not much older than my own teen. I spent my days rushing to courthouses speaking to their matters for my supervisors, evenings visiting clients at "my" correction centre (each student was assigned a jail in the Toronto area), before returning to the office to prepare for the next day. Finally, I'd lie in bed unable to sleep, fearing that my son might become a client of the firm due to my neglect. Was the cost of 'getting ahead' and making a good life in Canada being made at the expense of my son? There'd been years of overtime, studying at night, on weekends, and the crazy seventy-plus hours a week of articling needed to secure a job. That was my life as a single, Black mother. Perhaps I could have worked less, like other students at the firm, but they were white and confident of their abilities and intelligence. I was none of those and needed to compensate. For which of those, you ask? Most certainly the latter, but I believed that I needed to work harder and be a better citizen than my white counterparts. Of course, that was impossible—and exhausting. Still, I continued because it was a proven formula for at least some success.

After articling, I decided to move from Toronto. My son was heading south, to the United States, on a scholarship, while Clive and I would head west and eventually north in his aging, rusted-out Volkswagen car laden with our essential possessions in Rubbermaid containers. With cross-country skis strapped to the roof we started our journey across Canada, through those provinces my finger had traced on my son's globe years earlier in England.

Everyone should experience the horizontal snow of prairie blizzards powered by winds so strong that you wonder whether the car will be caught up in a vortex and dropped in a farmer's field miles away. We moved on from Regina, after the blizzard had left tractor trailers lying in the ditch like stranded turtles. I was in awe of Mother Nature then and again when the mirage suspended above the horizon morphed into the Rocky Mountains. It seemed an age before they swallowed us up. We almost ended our search for a new home in Canmore, but the North kept whispering in my ear, "You promised you'd spend at least a winter in the Yukon."

It was -42°C when we arrived in Whitehorse in January, making a mockery of my Gore-Tex jacket and every layer of clothing I'd squeezed beneath it. I lay on the bed that night staring at the electrical plates and the motel door trimmed, like tinsel, with hoarfrost. The next day, my hair and eyelashes froze as we walked three blocks to Main Street to find arctic gear. I clomped out of the store in heavy Sorel boots and fur-trimmed, down-filled parka, hood covering my face so that my gender and race were a mystery to others dressed in similar fashion.

My only preparation before leaving Toronto had been to write to my former boss in Whitehorse; I figured she'd allow me to rent space in her offices and set up my own practice. Her lack of response before we left Toronto didn't concern me.

By April, we were desperate. I dreamt of debt collectors with machetes chasing me for my student loans.

My former boss had moved from the Yukon shortly before we arrived. Though Clive and I had delivered résumés and followed up with calls, we had no job prospects and funds were dwindling rapidly. We talked about moving on to Yellowknife, undeterred by the fact that neither of us had visited the place or knew anyone who lived there. Days later, I was offered a position with two lawyers in Whitehorse. The following week Clive was employed.

Sir, you'd have laughed if you were a spectator in the courtroom watching my first appearance as a lawyer. It had been at least two years since I'd been in court as an articling student. In Toronto, I was just one of hundreds of students and lawyers speaking in court; in Whitehorse, I could not lose myself in numbers. It was important that I make a good impression on the judge and other lawyers. My voice wobbled as I spoke to the judge and I gripped the podium to conceal my shaking hands. It wasn't my best performance, but my client emerged victorious. I still recall the judge's quiet patience and the congratulatory words from the lawyers who would become my colleagues. It's been my experience in the Yukon that as a lawyer you're judged not by the colour of your skin but by your abilities and your behaviour—towards your peers, clients, the judge, and the Court's staff. I wish that, as part of this progress report, I could state that this has always been the case, but that wouldn't be accurate.

Sir, my legal background compels me to offer evidence that racism still exists in Canada, despite people assuring me that it doesn't, or if it does, it's rare. Only a couple of weeks ago, a friend on Facebook shared her young son's first experience of racism in Toronto. He was told by one of his friends that he couldn't join in a game because his skin was too dark. How did that child's peers come to judge him in that manner? Is there any parent of colour who hasn't braced themselves for that experience? My son's first experience—or the first he shared with me—happened when we still lived in Toronto. He was a gangly tween sitting on a park bench staring vacantly (gormlessly is the English expression, as I recall) into space. A police car pulled up and the two officers questioned him—*What are you doing here? What's your name? What's in your bag? Where do you live?* They followed him in their car as he walked home. I wanted to weep as he said, "I felt like a criminal, but I wasn't doing anything wrong, Mom." Son, it was me who did you wrong by not preparing you for that first time.

I was mistaken for an accused person more than once while I was an articling student. Not even my smart Jones New York pastel outfit with complementing shoes and jacket and my butter-soft leather Columbian briefcase could protect me from the Court clerk's belief that I was an accused, waiting for my case to be heard. "Stay behind the gate until your case is called. Only your lawyer is allowed up here." I was too embarrassed and humiliated to defend myself. My boss rushed to my defense, berating the woman for her error. She glared at me sitting beside him at the counsel table, as if she still doubted my innocence despite his harsh recriminations. The next time, in a different courtroom, the clerk was so mortified by her mistake that I found myself comforting her and reassuring that I took no offence. Too often, I've reacted as if I was responsible for another's stereotypical assumptions.

There were few Black people or other people of colour when I moved to Whitehorse. While that has changed, it's still the kind of place where, as a Black person approaches, we'll either acknowledge each other by a nod and slight raise of the eyebrows as we pass, or deliberately avert our eyes as if we haven't seen each other.

Because there were so few Black people when I arrived in the 1990s, I felt like a Black pioneer in the Yukon. It turns out that close to 3,500 African-American soldiers came before me during World War II, literally carving out and paving the Alaska Highway, the route that Clive and I drove to reach the Yukon. Many came from the southern States to northern British Columbia, the Yukon, and Alaska, working in temperatures that dropped as low as -55°C and harsh conditions to build the supply route. It's oddly comforting to know that I'm by no means the first Black person to visit these communities.

Sometimes I think of what I would have missed if we hadn't emigrated: howling wolves at night in Algonquin Park; soaring bald eagles over the Yukon River in search of fish; encountering the black bears and grizzly bears; hearing the frenzied sounds of dozens of dog teams waiting to start the Yukon Quest; gliding on cross-country skis in the night with only a headlight to guide your way; gazing up into the night skies at so many stars that it appears as if children have tossed glitter into the air; watching northern lights dance to the music of the universe. I don't regret my decision to leave behind the country I was born and raised in.

My time in the North might be coming to an end. Like others who've moved south, I want to be closer to family, to my son who now lives in Vancouver. I'm overthinking, analyzing, recording the pros and cons of an urban life in British Columbia. Am I ready to leave the Yukon? How will my husky dog adapt to confined off-leash areas bounded by chain-link fencing? How will I adapt to less open wilderness where you can be lost for days? And I'm concerned that I will be starting again in one important respect: being accepted as a Black person. It seems to me that western Canada lags well behind the Toronto area in its acceptance of Black culture, despite people of colour moving there in increasing numbers. In the two years since my son moved to Vancouver, he's been fired from a job because he was Black, another first for him. I feel responsible, Sir—I encouraged him to move west for purely selfish reasons, without considering the environment he'd be entering. I worry that he'll be stopped and questioned by police without reason, or worse. We take bigger risks than our white counterparts when we uproot and move elsewhere or even when we visit new places. Sometimes those risks pay off and sometimes there are more obstacles to navigate than we anticipated.

Lately, I've had a vague urge to retire from my well-paid job as a negotiator with the local government, sell or store most of my possessions, sell the house, pack what the dog and I absolutely need in my old Rubbermaid containers, and head out on the Alaska Highway in my minivan. I've always wanted to see Anchorage and Denali National Park. Eventually I'll run out of road and turn south. Perhaps by then I'll be ready to settle down. It's a half-formed, half-baked idea. Given my history, it's a distinct possibility.

Perhaps my next progress report will be written from Alaska, but Newfoundland is just as likely. There is still so much of Canada to explore. I can assure you though, Sir, I won't wait another thirty-eight years to provide a further progress report—unless it's possible to communicate from the other side.

With my warmest regards from Canada,

Christina Brobby

LETTERS TO
COMMUNITY

DIASPORIC
NARRATIVES

LIVED EXPERIENCES OF
CANADIANS OF AFRICAN DESCENT
IN RURAL NEW BRUNSWICK

— *Mary Louise McCarthy* —

*We acknowledge that the ancestors speak to us
in a place beyond written history.*
—bell hooks

am a seventh generation woman of African descent whose ancestors
were brought to the province of New Brunswick as property. This essay
will discuss the challenges of diasporic identities and the challenges
of occupying space in a colonized land. I will discuss how my ancestors
negotiated their spaces of settlement and negotiated their areas of con-
testation. These settlers of the Black diaspora arrived in New Brunswick
via two main routes. One route of arrival was as slaves who accompanied
the United Empire Loyalists in the late 1700s, and the second route was
as free Blacks coming to Atlantic Canada from the United States and

West Indies. As stated in Spray, "with the arrival of the loyalists came the first free Blacks to settle in New Brunswick." (1972, 15)

How do you explain your home, when you do not fit in with the dominant society? This is a consistent thread of colonialism that asked racialized people constantly to define who they are, or where were they born, or what country they are from? Colonialism comes with a sense of rupturing identities, dissected with a sense of non-belonging. Dionne Brand states,

> There is a sense in the mind of not being here or there, of no way out or in. As if the door had set up its own reflection. Caught between the two we live in the Diaspora, in the sea in between. Imagining our ancestors stepping through these portals one senses a surreal place, an inexplicable space. One imagines people so stunned by their circumstances, so heartbroken as to refuse reality. Our inheritance in the Diaspora is to live in this inexplicable space. (2001, 20)

Even in my earliest memories, I was aware of a difference within my family. I guess I could define my subtle young, sensing mind as being aware of the 'inside' or 'private' conversations that were spoken between my parents and elders. Was this a strategy of settlement or survival?

These conversations were always prefaced with, "What I am about to say is not to be repeated outside of this house." Now, as an adult and reflecting on our household norms, I see these tactics as a strategy of survival and protection.

I remember incidents that remind me that my family never fit in. These memories are of racism, brutality, and extreme aggression. One such incident was a horrendous attack on my brother. My brother was lured outside a bar in rural Maine and was beaten so badly that today he walks with a limp. I believe our family was in shock. When I first saw my brother, he was in a hospital bed suspended with traction. This brother was one year older than me, so I would imagine the incident happened around 1970. I assume the whole family was traumatized. Of course, now, forty years later, I am angry.

Did my parents' level of survival in a colonized society suggest such strategies as 'turning the other cheek'?

How does one turn the other cheek with such a heinous attack on your family? My parents are both deceased, but to my current knowledge, there was no police investigation or criminal action due to the incident that happened in the United States. Were my parents afraid, or did they want to move forward and put the incident behind them?

We are a large family, nine children, and my mother worked part-time and my dad was on a military pension. I recall in the summer of 2010 asking one of my aunts about the incident. I began to describe the incident in detail from memory. My aunt stated this was the first time she had heard of the incident, so judging from my aunt's reaction, I concluded that my parents truly had put the matter to rest.

In preparing my thoughts for this paper, I chose to share that specific incident to demonstrate the spaces and experiences of discontentment. It is clear that the on-going desires of most marginalized groups, and my family specifically, are to move forward in their lives and prepare a safe environment for their children. That specific incident of violence and racism can be called a rupture. I would hasten to suggest, for my parents, experiencing this violent act towards their child would be a reminder that in many ways we, African descendants, will never fit in, but it also raises the question, would my family want to 'fit in' or would they rather want to be 'accepted' as equal members of society?

I am a child of another generation. Perhaps I am different than my family members because of the way I was raised. I was taught to suppress my feelings. Those ruptures change me. I am no longer shut down, nor am I prone to suppressing my emotions. As a mother myself, I have not raised my son in a style similar to my parents. Specifically, and perhaps as a result of what I have experienced, I am constantly analyzing life, analyzing expressions, and analyzing the communications of all peoples. I am a critical theorist. I often ask myself, are we naive enough to not think that these settlement struggles of Black Canadians are built on a bloody foundation? These bloody foundations are the multiple experiences and traumas associated with oppression and racism that my ancestors dealt with on a daily basis as they lived their lives and attempted to cohabitate in this province of New Brunswick.

A site of sacred space, the African Methodist Episcopal (AME) church, built in 1893, was a site of community, of profit, as well as a space that my ancestors built, owned, and maintained. As well, I would like to put forth the suggestion that the AME Church was the nucleus of the African community, the community of which I am a proud descendant. I see the church as an area of resistance to colonialism, and a space that was owned and maintained by an inner circle of elders. This community of African descendants, my relatives, worked to keep this church alive and to maintain a safe place for all members. In doing so, they often held evening musical groups, such as women's choirs, men's choirs, quilting groups, social teas—all efforts to keep a sense of togetherness for the community. As a site of resistance, this community and church provided a gathering of like-minded souls to show support and share strategies. Individuals could share their experiences of racism and prejudice so that others would be mindful and aware of those particular individuals who did not treat our community members with respect.

This church also served as a meeting place. Ironically, it became a meeting place for all people as the music concerts were discussed up and down the central river valley of New Brunswick. My ancestors did not charge admission, however they did pass around an offering, and it was clear that all members of society frequented the AME Church concerts. The talent of the church congregation was used to financially support and maintain the building for many years to come. Sadly, the demographic of the Black community shifted after the Second World War. The AME Church building was sold in the 1960s due to a dwindling membership. The AME church had a lifespan of over fifty years of positive experiences.

What has been a gift to me is that the memories of this church will live on in the New Brunswick Provincial Archives. I have been able to donate some items that my mother had left amongst her personal papers to the archives. These documents will provide a record of this church that will be forever digitalized and incorporated into the archival history of this AME Church and bear witness to the church's rightful place in New Brunswick history. As a descendant of this community and this church I feel very proud and excited about this particular part of our ancestors' contribution to the fabric and development of the province of New Brunswick. The documents donated include the original deed of the church, a minute book for the women's group called The Coloured Willing Workers Club, and a brief essay on the building and construction of the church that began in 1893.

The space created by the AME Church community was and is a metaphoric space of belonging. I would argue the sense of belonging was a direct result of the sense of community that was built, fostered, and protected on the AME Church grounds initially, and later in our oral history. Our oral history has been passed down to the descendants of the AME Church, of which I am now an elder. It is my wish to use this paper as one of the vehicles, alongside my PhD, to tell my ancestors' stories. These stories are shared as a way to build community and mentor the community as they adapt and grow. The shared spirituality of my ancestors is another voice that I feel called to advocate for. In this research, one area that I am compelled to address in particular is my ancestors' segregated graves.

Based on my observation, my ancestors were segregated in their death. Is this a demonstration of binarisms to see that, in one instance, the church was a space of community and a source of pride for my ancestors, and then, in another, my ancestors' bodies were segregated in an isolated section of the community graveyard?

In keeping with this notion of not belonging that I suggest is supported by the physical segregation of my ancestors' graves, I will refer to Dionne Brands' *A Map to the Door of No Return*. As she writes, "our inheritance in the Diaspora is to live in this inexplicable space" (2001, 20). My ancestors were constantly reminded that they did not belong, but existed in this inexplicable space—the forced migration of my ancestors from their African homes—and then were attempting to live their lives in harmony in a new country, with few tools to survive other than their determination and their spiritual guidance. Katherine McKittrick explains the concept of diasporic space: "Questions of home, nation, ethnicity and violence have also been used to clarify the African or black diaspora" (2009, 156). To elaborate on this quote is to define our experiences as Africans in a new land and our struggles of settlement, community, and home.

Recently, as I walked the burial fields of my ancestors, I was saddened to see where their graves are physically located. These graves, dating back to the 1800s, were segregated in isolated parts of the graveyard, separate from the main population. In one cemetery, my ancestors' graves are situated on a hill facing the river. In another, the graves are all at one end of the property. The older graves have fallen down. I have been informally researching their burial grounds and asking questions, hoping to secure a map of the original design of the graveyard.

When I emailed a gentleman, Wallace Hale, who was responsible for cataloguing many of the graves in the province of New Brunswick, he stated that he did not recall any segregation, certainly not any intentional segregation. Hale felt if there was segregation, it was due to the cost of the plots. Hale had catalogued over six thousand New Brunswick graves in the 1980s. Hale stated in an email:

> Obviously, it didn't register with me that the Methodist Cemetery was a "back of the bus" affair. I'm still not satisfied that it was by deliberate design, but was perhaps due to the back plots being more affordable.
>
> Still, I do know the KKK had an active chapter at one time in Woodstock, although they seem to have done little other than burn a cross on the Grafton hill in the 1920s or '30s. I think a look at the cemetery map is essential and I'll try to confirm if it's in my possession. (Personal email correspondence, December 9, 2010)

This correspondence illustrates the experiences of settlement issues that arise out of a society that views my ancestors as second-class citizens.

Although Hale does suggest it is about economical disparities, again, this is another strategy of control, highlighting the issue of who sets the prices for the gravesites. I would say that certainly my ancestors would not be at the table for those discussions. My purpose in bringing these experiences to light is to explain that as members of the Black diaspora, we were so very isolated in rural New Brunswick.

Another example of unbelonging: through my PhD research I have become aware that an entire Black graveyard has actually been abandoned and is now under water. I was shocked to become aware of the former graveyard submerged beneath one of the main rivers in New Brunswick. This river, the Saint John River, flows through the central part of the province. My ancestors' graves were located at the far end of the cemetery, closest to the water. In the mid- to late 1960s, a large water dam was built, and in preparing the land, homes and communities were relocated. No one was there to advocate for these graves. I was shocked to read in the files of the New Brunswick Electric Power Commission that many were left and they are now under the Saint John River. What was more distressing is that over 100 of those graves were of my ancestors, the early African settlers of New Brunswick, most notably my great-grandfather. His name was listed as one of the ancestors buried in that graveyard. Angry and determined to make amends for this hurtful injustice to my community, I am still writing and researching, in addition to approaching big business to address the wrong that has been done.

While the management behind the power dam built a monument to pay respect to the graves that were relocated, the monument was also done in a haphazard way without any consultation with the community. The deceased were listed with only their last names recorded and no dates of birth or death. As well, the monument itself was segregated physically in a solitary space in a new graveyard. I have in my possession copies of the blueprints of the new graveyard where the monument was installed in the mid-1960s with an implicitly segregated section for the Black graves. It does not get much clearer than that! I also have evidence that the management chose to use only last names for this memorial stone in order to save money on the inscribing costs. It is so very sad and so very wrong to do this injustice to these individuals, my ancestors, who worked so hard to find safety and shelter, only to be disrespected in death.

I present these experiences as un/settling experiences. A society that is built on racism and colonialism, of course, is a society composed of individuals who have power and those who do not have power. However as Frantz Fanon states in his book, *Black Skin, White Masks*, "He who is reluctant to recognize me opposes me" (1967, 218). I wish to state that to live your life within the African diaspora is to encounter opposition on a daily basis. Simply put, the system of colonialism is riddled with racist attitudes and beliefs.

In closing, the title of this paper speaks to the issues of the constant challenges my ancestors were brought up against as they attempted to negotiate their lives. Brand (2001) has a powerful way of speaking of the past, reminding us we are descendants of the transatlantic slavery system. Brand says, "The horror is of course three or four hundred years of slavery, its shadow was and is colonialism and racism" (22). My wish is to not look back but to move forward with education and integrity, and place the memory of my ancestors into a positive light.

So, as a descendant of those strong, courageous people who struggled for survival and justice, I am here today grappling with my ancestral stories and attempting to make sense of my life and of my family memories. I am choosing to use the talents I have been blessed with to give back to my ancestors and dedicate my PhD work to their memory.

I believe I am being directed to do this work. I am a believer in unwritten, unspoken knowledges, or ways of awareness. bell hooks describes how we are connected and directed by our ancestors, and I, too, am a believer in myself and my individual strength, my DNA that supports me and propels me forward.

I believe also that for me, continued research into my ancestors' lives, work, and contributions to the province of New Brunswick is one of my main settlement strategies.

I will close with a quote from Joseph Drummond, who wrote the foreword of W.A. Spray's book, *The Blacks in New Brunswick*:

> We are a people who desire our Freedom, Justice, Equality and our Dignity. This work, a history of the Blacks in New Brunswick, is a partial attempt to rewrite a segment of the history of a strong people—the Black People. (1972)

REFERENCES

Brand, D. 2001. *A Map to the Door of No Return*. Toronto: Doubleday Canada.

DuBois, W.E.B. 1970. *The Gift of Black Folk: The Negroes in the Making of America*. New York: Washington Square Press.

Fanon, F. 1967. *Black Skin, White Masks*. Paris: Groce Press.

McKittrick, K. 2006. *Demonic Grounds: Black Women and the Cartographies of Struggle*. Minneapolis: University of Minnesota Press.

———. 2009. "Diaspora." In *International Encyclopedia of Human Geography, Volume 3* edited by R. Kitchen and N. Thrift, 151–161. Oxford: Elsevier.

Spray, W.A. 1972. *The Blacks in New Brunswick*. Fredericton: Brunswick Press.

PATERNAL
BLOOD MEMORY
VOLUME 1

— KYLA FARMER —

The world is a family.
One is a relative, the other stranger, Say the small-minded.
The entire world is a family, Live the magnanimous.
Be detached, be magnanimous, lift up your mind.
Enjoy the fruit of Brahmanic freedom.
—Maha Upanishad, 6.71–75

It's a tall bill, I usually say, or I ask them to guess, for fun and curiosity's sake—when people ask me where I'm from. Most of these interactions are annoying and a demonstration of society's ignorance and arrogance.

Sometimes I say, "From my mother's womb," and other times, "Earth," which is the truth, yet usually doesn't satisfy whatever exotic vacation destination they were expecting to hear me say.

Where I am from is a story that will take us on a journey all across the world, contradict and align itself in mind-bending ways, and ultimately, may give you a different lens on how to see human beings. A story about many people and many places.

I am on a mission to figure this all out. A lifelong mission, assembled from the crumbs and clues that made their way through time, passed down to me during my youth.

I have been putting the pieces together to help myself understand this fascinating and puzzling multi-dimensional identity of mine. I want to pass down this knowledge. This has been one of the most arduous and powerful things I have done for myself. My writings here will introduce you to me, a story I will continue to write over time as I learn and experience the truth of my family trees.

May this essay encourage you to think to yourself, what was destined for me to uncover within myself?

I AM

I was born on unceded and unsurrendered **Algonquin Territory**.
I am so grateful to the land, the people of the land, and their
 ancestors.
I have been guided by blood- and land-ancestors while
 navigating a colonial petrol state.

Born as a womxn who is of **Afrikan & European** descent, my
 creations reflect my intersections—
their beauties, wisdoms, complexities, stories, and urgencies for
right now and our collective future.

I believe in
the **liberation of Afrikan people worldwide;**
ending discrimination and the entire scope of violence &
 systemic oppression towards
**womxn, queer, trans, gender non-conforming & two-spirit
 peoples;**
the recognition, empowerment, and true reconciliation for

Indigenous people of Turtle Island and all over the world;
the stewardship of
land we live on, water we rely on for life, and air we breathe,
as keepers, settlers, & visitors;
the ability to appreciate **all forms of life—**
that flies, that swims, that walks, that we can't see or feel;
every person in the world having **knowledge and love of self,**
   family, community;
the way I speak and that I deserve to live in my **truth.**

I am a nomadic wild womxn constantly living between, outside of, and within multiple dimensions and worlds. I create resilient intersectional economies and build bridges of understanding within myself and between people. I am redefining what it means to work with purpose and in the arts. I lovingly and carefully do my best to love our blessed Mother Earth. I am love, a human, seeker of the truth.

I am a Farmer. I am Perry's daughter. I embody the Farmer Fire, as my family calls it. In 2017, Perry and I were fortunate enough to join our family's community in Jordantown, Acaciaville, and Conway, Nova Scotia, for a community reunion. It was life-changing: a return home for many across our villages' diaspora. After this communal return home, my father and I now talk about the Afrikan Nova Scotian community's realities and needs, we envision building a home on the road he spent time on as a kid and how we can contribute to the empowerment of Jordantown, Acaciaville, and Conway, Nova Scotia. It's a dream come true for the little girl in me, who saw this all in her mind's eye long ago. He hadn't been to Nova Scotia for almost fifty years before this reunion. After four years of visiting Nova Scotia on my own, reactivating a connection down home, and sharing those experiences with my father, his siblings, and mother, we were all together in our home-place away from home. This, I will be forever grateful for. This is joy. We, are joy.

Knowledge of self is powerful.

EMANCIPATION

My father's family has been on Mi'kmaq Territory, colonially known as Nova Scotia, since the 1700s, in Historic Black Communities of Afrikan Nova Scotians. I am so grateful to ancestors for constantly reminding me, even when I stood to forget, that I am the answer to their silent and sung prayers, their Afrofuture Vision. They toiled through the depths of hell on Earth for me to be who I am today. Such magikal, brilliant people, with traditions that transcend time, made of Cosmologik Wisdom.

AFRIKAN NOVA SCOTIAN PARENT

August 1st is the day my Afrikan Nova Scotian father was born. I cherish this day with all of my being. For without it, I wouldn't be. August 1st is the day that reminds me I know I am free. I walk like I am free. Talk like I am free. Love, smile, and feel free in a sovereign, empowered body, liberated soul, loving heart, and emancipated mind. August 1st is colonially known as Canada's 'Civic Holiday'—when it is actually the day celebrating the emancipation from slavery for people of Afrikan descent in the British colonies.

The 1833 Slave Emancipation Act did not come into force until August 1, 1834. The first step was the freeing of all children under six. However, although the many thousands of enslaved people in the British West Indies were no longer legally slaves after August 1, 1834, they were still made to work as unpaid apprentices for their former masters. These masters continued to ill-treat and exploit them. Enslaved people in the British Caribbean finally gained their freedom at midnight on July 31, 1838.[*]

My father grew up in Robinson-Huron Treaty territory, in the traditional territory of the Atikameksheng Anishnaabeg, colonially known as Sudbury, Ontario. Grandson of the last man hung in Nova Scotia, son of the man who had a baseball team called The Coloured Kings, a man with

---

[*] http://www.nationalarchives.gov.uk/pathways/blackhistory/rights/emancipation.htm

many siblings and a high respect and love for his mother. I will never know the extent of the hardships, discrimination, barriers, and challenges my father has faced, but I do know some of it. It goes long and deep, and most of it I have been able to learn language for as I got older, primarily as intergenerational trauma. My father has defeated so many odds I've lost count. He is a man who has made do with what he had, a wizard at creating opportunities for himself, a man with impeccable hustle and tools for survival, and a person who simply wants to enjoy life and the fruits of his labour. My father is the hardest-working person I will ever know. He has shown me what it means to grow as a person, to rise above your circumstances, to chart your own path, to believe in oneself, to believe that life can get better if you "work hard, and play harder." I am beyond grateful to be his firstborn, his daughter, and his legacy.

AFRIKAN NOVA SCOTIAN ANCESTOR

Jupiter and Venus Farmer. Names I heard of a few times growing up. Having been fascinated by space and planets since youth, I thought having ancestors with the names Jupiter and Venus was epic. One day, when I was twenty-eight, I googled Jupiter Farmer. There were a multitude of resources on the first page, mostly information on the website of the Black Loyalist Heritage Centre, which I visited about a year later. They had stories about him, his indentured labour agreement papers, his will and testament, and a vast pot of knowledge about the rest of my community. What a blessing! Here it was! The obscure place in the world where I can get the answers I need.

Since that day I have learned that Jupiter and Venus Farmer were folks entered in The Book of Negroes, as they were Black Loyalists who fought alongside the British Army in the American Revolutionary War of the late 1700s.

Jupiter, according to my research so far, was stationed or bound into the enclave of slavery in New Jersey. But, of course, my family has other stories, which makes me curious and intuitive to the fact that multiple information sources are true. I need to understand the rest of the story of how that is so. Venus lived in South Carolina before fleeing north to get free. Learning about that war, and slavery, from a completely different perspective outside of institutional education was essential in the understanding of history that I need. I need to know the perspectives of my people during a time where everything depended on us.

Where were our bodies and what we were doing? I am forever thankful and grateful to Jupiter and Venus Farmer, for having the courage to survive through the plantations, fighting in multiple wars alongside oppressors and against oppressors, and gaining more freedom for themselves, for my sake. What a love that is. What a blood memory that is.

They had intended on joining their community in the exodus to found Freetown, Sierra Leone; however, due to their indentured labour reality, were not permitted to go. I intend to continue that journey for them, and to seek where we are indigenous to, afterwards. Insha'Allah.

AFRIKAN NOVA SCOTIAN ELDER

Great-uncle Hubert Johnson is Canada's first Black chief warrant officer in the armed forces. An incredible community leader. He mentored and cared for over fifty youths in the community in the 1970s. He is King of the kitchen, garden, grill. He is King at clearing land, building homes, caring for burial grounds, and being a father, grandfather and great-grandfather.

Hubert has been the caretaker of the Afrikan Nova Scotian burial ground where his mother, my great-grandmother, Blanch Slaven's body rests. Located just outside of Digby there used to be an Afrikan Nova Scotian community called Brindleytown. I was told the coastal area near Brindleytown was called Negro Inlet—a fisheries community. Over the years, people guided by white supremacy and racism drove this community out and bought up the land.

Three houses, one business, and the burial ground are what remain of Brindleytown. What was it like for my great-uncle to go out there and maintain the grass, put up headstones for our families? He speaks of it with great pride and love, truly a labour of love and devotion. His care of this land in this way is iconic love in action.

Hubert first brought me to two burial grounds. It was very early in the morning, and we were set to drive hours east to Halifax so that I could catch the train to Montreal, and eventually back to Toronto. The morning dew and grey-blue sky, the quietness of the town, made for a peaceful introduction. First, he brought me to where our family is also buried, down the road and up the hill in the forest. I got to see the beautiful tree that was planted where his father and my grandmother's father, Arthur, rests. Arthur and Blanch's families, from what I know thus far, come from the Caribbean. We stop at a plot with soil that had recently been laid, where Hubert's beloved, Greta, rests.

We walk to her and Hubert says to me, "Now, I really want to be with her, every day, I miss her every day, I can still hear her talking to me. But I know I still have some things to do. I'll be with her again soon." Watching his eyes and hands, the same as my grandmother's, shapes and bends and opens my heart wide. Such a sweet love. I am beyond grateful that I was able to meet Greta during my first visit to Digby County. May her soul rest in peace, power, and love.

A short drive around the curved roads, we pulled up to the burial ground in what remains of Brindleytown. My great-uncle tells me the story about his life, and travelling, and returning home to see that there was no caretaker of the land where our family and community are buried. He wrote and received a grant to begin a decades-long commitment to take care of the land. The view when standing there is breathtaking, an inlet connected to the Bay of Fundy. Interestingly, in my youth I did an extensive project on the Bay of Fundy with a friend. Amazing how this is where my family has been all this time.

We walk around the area, looking to see if, amongst the few rocks and small stones with hand-carved letters on them, one of them bears the name of my great-grandmother, Blanch. Here she is! The woman whose name my father gave for my middle name. You have to look at the stone very hard and closely to be able to see that it is her name. I get to sit with her for the first time. I get to look at the water, and the sky and hills, the boats floating by, while visiting. What a blessing this is. Hubert and I enjoy silence while we breathe and are present with each other and those in our family tree. We look at each other, at the water stretching into the distance, at the ground. At this moment, it sinks into my deep currents how grateful I am to be here, finally, and how grateful I am to Blanch, and Hubert.

Grateful, to be.

Why are people in such denial of the present and historical realities of extreme racism, slavery, and systemic oppression towards Indigenous peoples of Turtle Island, and those of Afrikan descent, those who are foundational to present-day Canada? It is because of that that I was not able to know what my father's family stories are until I was almost thirty years old.

AFRIKAN NOVA SCOTIAN NEXT GENERATION

I have so many cousins. It absolutely blows my mind how brilliant they are and how much we love each other. A generation full of imagination, optimism, creativity, and knowledge. These are the people we all need to love, uplift, support, teach, encourage, foster, and most of all, allow them to be exactly whoever and however they want to be. I have cousins all over Turtle Island, on the Farmer and Johnson sides, and will continue to go to where I can to meet them and ensure that we continue to build relations, gather as often as we can, and continue on the legacy of our ancestors, guided by knowledge of self.

Meeting most of my cousins during the Community Reunion of 2017 was an immense blessing.

One cousin, ten years old, tall, daring, adventurous, has a penchant for filmmaking and knows the land where our family lives very well. I spent an entire day with her in the summer's sun listening to her knowledge of the land—following her lead as she described its vastness. She grew up being a part of the land, getting to know it, and having that part of her life be a sacred space for herself, a place where she could be herself and be free. I am so grateful to have been guided by her in this way. She brought us to a place in the road, past where Arthur rests, where a small creek passes underneath the road. We jumped onto the patch of sand that trails out of the tunnel into the water, took off our shoes, and off we went.

Travelling through this shallow brook, our feet were gliding over rocks in the water, feeling all the marine plant life slide along the bottom of our feet, a soothing texture on the blade-like layers of rock, hanging off branches that lean over the shallow water. I can still see the way the sunshine and the air played with the thick forest that surrounded us, and still hear all the animals around us. Such a delight to stand in the water with her, eyes wide open, feeling the sun on my face—to be still, and listen. She was bringing us to her favourite destination, waterfalls. We didn't make it that far that day, as there was the community reunion dinner to attend. "Next time I visit, let's go," I said. Her presence and essence reminded me that this is where I belong, this place in the diaspora, where my humanity, my face, my voice, is recognized.

AFRIKAN NOVA SCOTIAN AFROFUTURE

Comrades teach me about Afrofuturism, amongst many endless other things that free my mind, body, heart, and soul.

Scholars, narratives, hxstories, and histories teach me about a time past, what is urgent in the now, and possibilities for tomorrow. Self-teachings, knowledge shared in community, research, experiments, experiences, and my own wild and beautiful imagination teach me things about my family's history in Nova Scotia that obviously no school, institution could teach me. I am so blessed to be a part of the Johnson Family from Jordantown and the Farmer Family from Shelburne and Birchtown, Mi'kmaq Territory. My intention is to be able to care for a small part of land our family's community is a part of, build a legacy home, designed in love with the Earth, that will also be an artist retreat centre, community space, and lodging for visitors.

Jupiter and Venus Farmer taught me to fight for freedom for myself and others, to keep faith for a brighter day even when it seems that all the odds are against you, and to have hope and move with that hope, even when you are stripped of your humanity. I am their seventh generation.

Indigenous peoples of Turtle Island have taught me so much about governance, ancestry, truth, beauty, and spirituality. I am grateful to have learned from Indigenous folks since youth, about the interconnectedness of nature and us, about living with the land, and most importantly, about acting in a way that is considerate and compassionate to at least seven future generations. I am grateful for every opportunity to share in and act on my affinity and love for water with Indigenous folks—they define how we all need to relate to water, the elixir of life. Water is life, *Mni Wiconi*.

So, brothers and sisters, what must we do—RIGHT NOW, forever and always—to give our Afrofuture children, and their Afrofuture children, the foundation for freedom in all ways, shapes, forms, and means, and ends?

Can you hear me? Do you overstand?

I hope. I pray. I know. I do not know. It is written. *El Mektoub*.

Giving thanks as the sojourn continues...

Righteousness is not that you turn your faces toward the east or the west, but [true] righteousness is [in] one who believes in Allah, the Last Day, the angels, the Book, and the prophets and gives wealth, in spite of love for it, to relatives, orphans, the needy, the traveler, those who ask [for help], and for freeing slaves; [and who] establishes prayer and gives zakah; [those who] fulfill their promise when they promise; and [those who] are patient in poverty and hardship and during battle. Those are the ones who have been true, and it is those who are the righteous.

—Al-Qur'an al-Kareem [The Noble Qur'an],
Surah Al-Baqarah, 2:177

ON HAUNTED PLACES

ENCOUNTERING SLAVERY IN QUEBEC

— *Délice Mugabo* —

State terror against Black communities in Canada and elsewhere is fairly well documented—in fact, we can even see how debates about systemic racism still don't take into account white citizenry terror. Yet, white Québecois—some as members of an organized white supremacist group, but most not—inflicted a particular kind of violence on Black women, men, and children through the 1990s, the period that I studied during my graduate research. Stories of white citizen terror also reveal how, despite the general lack of knowledge about the history of slavery here, white Québec society is still able to mobilize an associated set of knowledge that animates routine manifestations of white supremacy and anti-blackness. In other words, not knowing the details of slavery and its systematic dehumanization of Black peoples has not hampered the ability to register Blackness in terms of fungibility and submission to white domination. So, even if Black people living in Québec today are not necessarily descended from those who were enslaved here, since the history of slavery ties Africa to the 'Old' and 'New' Worlds in violent ways, we arrive in Québec already being part of this society that slavery created.

I explore here—through the works of Saidiya Hartman and other Black feminist scholars—the many ways in which Black people in Montreal continue to be haunted by the specific forms of captivity that have marked Black bodies across the Atlantic. To do so, I offer a reading of the story of Botche Kafe—a former Black teacher in various East-End Montreal high schools for twenty years until the mid-1990s. Kafe's story blatantly exposes the blurred line that exists between enslavement and enslaveability. To be clear, my goal is not to claim the lives of the Black women, men, and children who were enslaved in Québec as our own, but to reveal how their lives and our lives are linked today. Québec society, as we live it today, is part of the world that slavery created.

FOR THE DEAD, THE DYING, AND THOSE LONGING FOR LIFE

New France is a former slave-holding, white, settler colony that was first used for resource extraction (mainly fish and fur). As its role moved from extraction to settlement, successive colonial administrators lobbied the French crown to allow them to import African slaves (Viger and Lafontaine 1859, 2). Although a great majority of slaves under the French regime were Indigenous peoples from the western borderlands in present-day Wisconsin, Illinois, or Ohio, historians number enslaved Black people to over a quarter of the enslaved population, or over one thousand. While enslaved Black people were usually brought in from the Caribbean, others were brought to New France as bounties of various wars waged in the United States, and newer records allude to ships arriving in New France directly from Africa carrying enslaved Black people (Gay 2004, 82). In her work on slavery in Québec, Charmaine Nelson explains that most enslaved Black people in New France arrived here through several crossings, at least two, if not more.

Christina Sharpe's (2016) masterful new book, *In the Wake*, begins by having us sit with the fact that the Black women, men, and children who did not survive these crossings—whether because of suicide or murder—still have a physical presence. Sharpe helps us understand the "time of slavery" (Hartman 2002) not just metaphorically but also materially. The idea that the time of slavery has not passed may be difficult for some; however, it becomes more difficult to refute when we are confronted with the fact that traces of enslaved Black bodies are still in the ocean. Sharpe recounts the story of the *Zong*, a slave ship that brought captives from Africa to Jamaica, 130 of whom were thrown overboard along the way. Sharpe reflects on what happened to their bodies in the ocean and carefully attends to how these men and women are actually still present. It is worth quoting her at length:

> It is likely, then, that those Africans, thrown overboard, would have floated just a short while, and only because of the shapes of their bodies. It is likely, too, that they would have sunk relatively quickly and drowned relatively quickly as well. And then there were the sharks that always traveled in the wake of slave ships. There have been studies done on whales that have died and have sunk to the seafloor.
>
> These studies show that within a few days the whales' bodies are picked almost clean by benthic organisms—those organisms that live on the seafloor....What happened to the bodies? By which I mean, what happened to the components of their bodies in salt water? Anne Gardulski tells me that because nutrients cycle through the ocean...the atoms of those people who were thrown overboard are out there in the ocean even today....The amount of time it takes for a substance to enter the ocean and then leave the ocean is called residence time. Human blood is salty, and sodium, Gardulski tells me, has a residence time of 260 million years. And what happens to the energy that is produced in the waters? It continues cycling like atoms in residence time. We, Black people, exist in the residence time of the wake, a time in which everything is now. It is all now. (Sharpe 2016, 40–41)

By invoking the Black lives that remain in the sea, Sharpe encourages us to consider how the residence time of enslaved Black women and men who died at sea can be paralleled to the anti-blackness that marks the wake of slavery. Sharpe's book reads like a prayer, a prayer for Black people, the dead, the dying, and those longing for life. Tying her own family loss to the reality of premature Black death—from the earthquake in Haiti, to police killings in the United States, to Black migrants dying in the Mediterranean Sea—Sharpe writes about anti-blackness as the fact of living in the wake of slavery. Let us return to that temporal marker—the "long time" of slavery—in a moment.

Dionne Brand is another Black feminist thinker whose work challenges us to centre slavery in our understandings of contemporary Black life. Her writings are particularly salient for the ways that they often place Black Canadian lives at the centre of the intricate geographies of the Black diaspora. In her novel *At the Full and Change of the Moon*, Brand (1999) demonstrates how the historical memory of slavery resurfaces as/ because of the recurring forms of violence that Black people in Canada experience. In the novel she tells the story of Marie Ursule, an enslaved Black woman in Trinidad who foresees leaving the memory of her life in the bones of her great-grandchildren who migrate to Canada in exile nearly a century after her death. Their great-grandmother's memories manifest themselves differently in each of their lives. Bola, for example, experiences her great-grandmother's trauma "not only [as] a psychological concept," but as "a culturally-transmitted marker of communal history and experience" (Johnson 2004, 2). For Brand, trauma results from a silenced collective history, including through individual stories stricken from archival records. 'Unforgetting' is what Brand calls the process of recovering these experiences. As she explains, it is "an endeavor of collective, interpersonal memory," a matter of "permitting history to arise where immediate understanding may not" (Johnson 2004, 3).

Having also interrogated the topic of collective memory, Toni Morrison explains that social memory is not just about history, but also about haunting (Gordon 2008). This is a theme that she explores in her 1987 novel, *Beloved*.

Inspired by the story of Margaret Garner, a Black woman who escaped slavery and kills her infant daughter in order to avert her child's re-enslavement by slave catchers who capture them. The book tells the story of how that daughter, Beloved, returns to Margaret several years later in the form of a ghost. By setting the story in 1873, ten years after emancipation, Morrison draws attention to how slavery had ended in name only. What we learn from *Beloved* is that "haunting is one way in which abusive systems of power make themselves known and their impacts felt in everyday life, especially when they are supposedly over and done with or when their oppressive nature is denied" (Gordon 2008, xvi).

Finally, Saidiya Hartman is another thinker whose work challenges our sense of historical memory. Hartman (2002) develops the concept of the "time of slavery" to refer to the dispossession that is an inheritance from slavery. In her argument Hartman clarifies that she does not mean that racism is unchanging. Rather, anti-blackness is intransigent and "one's condition is still defined largely by one's membership in the subject group" (2002, 776).

Similarly, Hartman also uses the concept of the "afterlife of slavery" to describe the ways in which "Black lives are still imperiled and devalued by a racial calculus and a political arithmetic that were entrenched centuries ago" (2007, 6). In sum, Hartman writes, "racial subjection, incarceration, impoverishment and second-class citizenship: this is the legacy of slavery that still haunts us" (2002, 766).

Taken together, Sharpe, Brand, Morrison, and Hartman allow us to reflect on the memory of slavery, how it is embodied and how it is carried. We learn that "anti-Black violence and stolen life define the very foundation of the settler state" (Hartman 2016, 210), and they tell us to "beware forgetting the enslavement or domination that persists and that often masquerades as emancipation or freedom" (Gordon 2008, 184).

This conceptual material helps us make sense of the various forms of anti-black violence that continue to mark Black life in Québec, and Botche Kafe gives us a snapshot of 1990s Montreal.

MR. KAFE'S CLASS: ANTI-BLACK VIOLENCE
IN QUÉBEC'S HIGH SCHOOLS

As with Dionne Brand, for whom the process of unforgetting is an integral part of creating and preserving a collective memory, Avery Gordon (2008) argues that the sociality of a place contains its own memories that linger over time. In this sense, it is very possible to arrive in a place and "bump into a rememory that belongs to somebody else" (Gordon 2008, 166). I would argue that Québec has its own memories of slavery that, together with other histories of slavery in the Atlantic world, merge to constitute part of the global history of anti-black violence and Black resistance. Botche Kafe's story is one where the experience of captivity in Ghana meets its contemporary equivalent in Québec.

Botche Kafe is a Ghanaian-born educator who taught at almost all of the high schools in the Laurentides region, just north of Montreal (Gagnon 1993). Having endured fifteen years of racial attacks from students at the Deux-Montagnes School Board, the fifty-four-year-old teacher submitted a complaint to the Québec Human Rights Commission in 1992, as the situation had caused "depression and anxiety so severe that it incapacitated him from working" (Ruggles and Rovinescu 1996, 94). Kafe kept several letters from his students and he presented them at the Human Rights Tribunal. "My mother is a racist," wrote one student, "here is her phone number. She's going to tell you all about racism. She's going to sock you." Another added, "You're supposed to be my slave not my teacher, haven't you see Roots?" (Ruggles 1993, 6). He testified that over the years students brought their excrement to throw at him (Ruggles and Rovinescu 1996) and had kicked him around in the classroom shouting: "If the nigger dies what does it matter?" and, "Nigger crisis...the niggers are everywhere" (Knowles 1996, 300). Students at the high school in Oka mocked Kafe "by doing African-style dances, feigning [drums] playing on their desks, and repeatedly telling him to go back to Africa" (Picard 1993, A5).

What later became disturbing to Black community members was that the school board had been trying to get rid of him since he began working for them. Kafe testified that "the board went out of its way to make his life unbearable—he was given an impossible course load in violation of the collective agreement; he was given students with behaviour problems and he never had the support of the administration" (Ruggles 1993, 6).

In 1984, students at Sainte-Eustache High School were taking bets on how long it would take to get Kafe to leave. Kafe testified in great detail about the ordeal that he went through (Ruggles and Rovinescu 1996).

> The principal also supported a student who gave me blows all the way from the third floor to his own office on the ground floor. He also refused to punish the student who flooded my classroom with fire extinguishers shouting "Drown the nigger"...and held my tie and pulled me around like a dog....The horrible barbaric things he [the principal of one of the schools] did to me are beyond description...like my whole self was destroyed by what was going on there. (Knowles 1996, 300)

The racist attacks took their toll on Kafe's mental health, and in 1990 he took a two-year sick leave. The school board then took measures to have him laid off. They appointed a psychiatrist who declared Kafe to be paranoid and suffering from delusions. Kafe was fired on that basis. It was then that he decided to submit a complaint to the Québec Human Rights Commission. In an interview a few years later, Kafe revealed that it was when students referred to him as a slave that he decided to fight back, for it invoked ancestral memories that he grew up with in Ghana.

Through their oral traditions people in his village still recount the stories of the raids made by the slave traders. The family story told about his great-great-grandmother is that she, along with everyone else, fled when the slave traders came to their village. But remembering that she had forgotten her cotton—the work that kept women occupied—she returned to the village to retrieve it and was captured and taken into slavery (Knowles 1996, 301).

Once, as an adult, Kafe visited a slave castle on the coast of Ghana where the enslaved were detained until they were taken away on the ships. One thing he still remembered from that visit was that "the last stop on African soil for slaves was the false floor of the castle which gave way so that the slaves fell onto the ships. Some would die at this point or fall on, and kill someone else" (Knowles 1996, 301). During his years living in the United States, Kafe visited important sites of slavery in the South, viewing from the other side of the Atlantic what he considered to be his own family history.

Black people from the continent are often said to have no memory of or interest in the history of slavery and the fact that, generation after generation, the story of how Kafe's great-great-grandmother was captured by slave traders should make us pause and reflect on why it was so important for his family to preserve that memory. I can't help but see the parallels between Kafe's great-great-grandmother and Dionne Brand's Marie-Ursule, who planted her stories as an enslaved Black women into the memories of her grandchildren and beyond, anticipating that they will need them as they confront anti-black violence when they move to Canada. The story of Kafe and that of Marie-Ursule's descendants in Canada bring us to consider how "the routing of traumatic memory through interconnected lives and the ghosts that haunt them serves to unforget traumatic history by revealing its constant resonance in the present" (Johnson 2004, 13). In other words, Black diasporic history manifests itself in particular ways when, through collective forms of memory, the past reveals itself to still be present. Kafe's brutal experiences of anti-black violence—it must be noted, primarily at the hands of white children, therefore revealing how this kind of terror has no "age of innocence"—trigger a process of unforgetting, in Brand's sense, that allows him to access a collective memory that not only exceeds Québec territory but also reveals how contemporary forms of anti-black violence within it are not confined in space or time.

The students' claims to this Black man's enslaveability are not due to their ignorance, quite the opposite. They didn't evoke the American TV show *Roots* simply to transpose American history to Québec, but, from the transcripts of the legal case and the media coverage, they seemed intent to make it clear to him either that slavery was as much a reality in Québec as it had been in the United States, or that if slavery hadn't existed in Québec, then it should have! Either way, it's clear that these Québécois children were convinced that white people *anywhere* could enslave Black people *everywhere*. So, whether these students even had basic knowledge about the history of slavery in Québec is irrelevant, because they were expressing a belief that slavery should persist and that Kafe was enslaveable whether or not his ancestors had been enslaved in Québec.

In their annual report in 1992, Amnesty International condemned Canada's mistreatment of Indigenous peoples and wrote at length about the abuse committed against Mohawks in the Montreal region. They reported cases of Mohawk men being severely beaten at the police station in Saint-Eustache (Bonhomme 1992, A4). I bring up the Mohawk resistance struggle in and around Kanehsatà:ke and an example of the attacks against Indigenous people in Montreal after the so-called Oka Crisis to underline how racist attacks in Québec do not happen outside of history. These attacks actually illuminate how history—colonialism and slavery—is still at work. Botche Kafe actually taught in Oka from 1988 to 1991(Norris 1993), a period that overlaps with the crisis. Hence, Oka is very much a site where the ongoing history of white settler colonialism and the afterlife of slavery have been unfolding.

Scholarly articles on the case of Botche Kafe have focused on the intensive psychiatric attention that was unleashed on him, and offered great insights on how psychiatry is enmeshed with colonial and racist power in Québec and Canada (Knowles 1996; Cheboud and France 2012). Indeed, "the medical plot" that Kafe revealed and that was eventually used against him should continue to be unpacked for it illustrates one of the ways that anti-black violence, and resistance against it, is regulated through criminalization and "spirit murder" (Williams 1991, 73).* Kafe

---

* On December 25, 1992, Kafe sent a seven-page letter to the mayor of Verdun, the Human Rights Commission, the Department of Education, and the Ministry of Cultural Communities in which he detailed the injustices he had endured from students and school officials and alerted them to the toll that anti-black violence takes on Black people living in Montreal (Ruggles...

connected his abuse to the ongoing colonial arrangements of Québec society and "the afterlife of slavery" (Hartman 2007). Innocence is a foundational myth of the Québec nation, and this province continuously denies or minimizes its history of slavery.

Despite the scholarly material's deft analysis of the relationship between psychiatry and racism, it still falls into a predictable pattern. For example, in her article critiquing the role of psychiatry in further perpetuating the violence that Kafe experienced at the hands of students and school officials, Caroline Knowles explains that "disruptive adolescents, unconcerned with the political correctness of official 'multi-culturalism,' could shout 'burn the nigger,' voicing the feelings of an adult world which dared not" (Knowles 1996, 300). There is a way in which critiques of racism in psychiatry discharge Kafe but also exonerate his many aggressors. What has Québec white society "dared not" say or do to Kafe or other Black people? Analyzing the white students' violent actions as 'politically incorrect' isolated behaviour sets Kafe's experience in Montreal apart from the history of that place. The fact is that the white students who told Kafe that he should be their slave and not their teacher are part of the same community that had white

---

...and Rovinescu 1996). His letter was titled "Please help avoid a shooting rampage in Verdun." In it, Kafe explained that the Deux-Montagnes school board and their appointed psychiatrist organized a medical plot against him. Kafe then reminds his readers that previous cases of injustice had brought individuals to retaliate violently and publicly and that is why state officials must intervene against institutional racism. He recalled the case of a man who spent twenty-seven years trying to "tell the story of his trauma" but was ignored. The man, the letter states, went on to cut into pieces every human that came into sight. In the last paragraph, Kafe writes, "I am not anticipating any shooting rampage in Verdun, but everybody knows what provocations and injustice of this magnitude can do" (Ruggles 1993, 6). Arguing that the letter consisted of a death threat against Dr. Marc Guérin (the school board's psychiatrist whose office was in Verdun), Kafe was arrested, denied bail, jailed, and later detained at the Philippe Pinel Institute, a psychiatric hospital (Buckie 1993, A4).

mobs organized against Mohawk activists and community members during the 1990 Oka Crisis. There was no politically correct adult world distinct from "disruptive" white youth: all were part of an unrepenting white citizenry clear about Black and Mohawk unbelonging. In the case of Kafe, white youth at high schools in Oka and Sainte-Eustache were indeed reaffirming that place as a white-settled and slave-owning land. Not reckoning with the nature of racism and anti-blackness among white citizens—whether they hold positions of power or not—is part of what turns Black speech and Black resistance into a pathology. Clearly, white children too hold power over Black people.

It is no wonder that being called a slave in his classroom precipitated a series of family memories about his great-great-grandmother's capture by slave traders. What if Kafe's enslaved great-great-grandmother is among those who will continue to live in the sea for millions of years?

While it would be easy to assume that Kafe's foremother was brought to the United States, or perhaps to the Caribbean or South America, it's entirely possible that she was in New France, especially if we consider that the majority of enslaved Black people in Québec were sold in other colonies before their arrival here. Knowing that the slave route from the Continent to Québec was winding, we can better understand that enslaved Black people during the colonial era left memories in all of those places. The same can be said of Black people in Montreal today, whether they trace their origins to the Caribbean, to Africa, or to others parts of the Americas: the memories of slavery that they carry here are neither anachronistic nor displaced. On the contrary, these memories arrive in Québec and find a place because they 'bump into' ghosts that remember them.

CONCLUSION

Botche Kafe came to Québec with a familial and national history of slavery. His experience of anti-black violence here revealed the ties that linked Québec's history of slavery with his. He bumped into Québec's ghosts of slavery. These ghostly encounters compel us to refuse the linear narrative of progress that imposes itself in this so-called post-racial age. The "nonevent of emancipation" allows various forms of subjugation to shape the global landscape (Hartman 1997). Like Hartman, "I believe it requires us to rethink the meaning of abolition, not only as the not-yet, not simply as the event for which we are waiting, but as the daily practice of refusal and waywardness and care in the space of captivity, enclosure, and incarceration" (2016, 214).

REFERENCES

Bonhomme, J-P. 1992. "Amnesty International blâme le Canada pour le traitement réservé aux Mohawks." *La Presse*, July 9.

Brand, D. 1999. *At the Full and Change of the Moon.* New York: Grove Press.

Buckie, C. 1993. "Death-threat suspect is denied bail; Judge rules former teacher might be danger to society." *The Gazette*, June 3.

Cheboud, E., and M. Honoré France. 2012. "Counselling Black Canadians." In *Diversity, Culture and Counselling: A Canadian Perspective*, edited by M. Honoré France, M. del Carmen Rodriguez, G.G. Hett., 202–216. Edmonton: Brush Education.

Dunn, K. 1990. "International observers blocked by mob; Police do little to stop attacks by white mob, members charge." *The Gazette*, August 27.

Gagnon, M. 1993. "Deux-Montagnes: les commissaires invités à fermer le dossier de William Kafé." *La Presse*, April 28.

Gay, D. 2004. *Les Noirs du Québec, 1629–1900.* Québec: Les éditions du Septentrion.

Gordon, A.F. 2008. *Ghostly Matters: Haunting and the Sociological Imagination.* Minneapolis: University of Minnesota Press.

Hartman, S. 1997. *Scenes of Subjection.* New York: Oxford University Press.

———. 2002. "The Time of Slavery." *The South Atlantic Quarterly* 101 (4): 757–777.

———. 2007. *Lose our Mother: A Journey Along the Atlantic Slave Route.* New York: Farrar, Straus and Giroux.

———. 2016. "The Dead Book Revisited." *History of the Present* 6 (2): 208–215.

Horn, M. 1987. "Five Years of Terror." *U.S. News & World Report*, October 19: 75.

Johnson, E.L. 2004. "Unforgetting Trauma: Dionne Brand's Haunted Histories." *Anthurium: A Caribbean Studies Journal* 2 (1): article 4.

Knowles, C. 1996. "Racism and Psychiatry." *Transcultural Psychiatric Review* 33 (3): 297–318.

Norris, A. 1993. "Ruling cheers victim of racist harassment by pupils." *The Gazette*, April 17.

Picard, A. 1993. "Plagued by racist taunts, teacher awarded $10,000." *The Globe and Mail*, April 14.

Ruggles, C. 1993. "Hatred in the Classroom: The William Kafe Story." *Community Contact*, August 6.

———, and O. Rovinescu. 1996. *Outsider Blues: A Voice from the Shadows.* Halifax: Fernwood Publishing.

Saunders, P. 2008. "Defending the Dead, Confronting the Archive: A Conversation with M. NourbeSe Philip." *Small Axe* 12 (2): 63–79.

———. 2008. "Fugitive Dreams of Diaspora: Conversations with Saidiya Hartman." *Anthurium: A Caribbean Studies Journal* 6 (1): article 7.

Sharpe, C. 2016. *In the Wake: On Blackness and Being.* Durham, NC: Duke University Press.

Williams, P. 1991. *The Alchemy of Race and Rights.* Cambridge, MA: Harvard University Press.

THE PLACE THAT IS SUPPOSED TO BE SAFE

— ANGELA WRIGHT —

She pulled out a large sheet of paper and stuck it on the wall. Skin on the back of her hand rippled down to her wrist. The cane she used to prop herself up when she walked was leaning against the desk.

The assignment was simple: students had to uncover their cultural heritage. She went around the room one by one, asking her eight-year-old students to declare where their families came from. One country per line, with a check mark for every repetition. England, Wales, Scotland, the countries that occupied the greatest amount of space; a common occurrence across the French immersion classrooms of the burgeoning four- and five-bedroom community. Her eyes drifted to me and I mumbled, "Greece and Bermuda."

She backed away from the wall, still holding the marker in her hand. Turning to her students, she declared, "I am from Kanata."

How can she be from Kanata? I wondered. *That is not a country.* Kanata was a sprawling suburb in the west end of Ottawa undergoing massive development. Many of the homes were still under construction so I knew she was too old to be from there.

Madame Leclerc, a stout woman with a voice that bellowed across the classroom, belonged to a group of people called the Haudenosaunee, which the French renamed the Iroquois.

They were one of the many peoples who lived in Canada—before it was Canada. She explained that in her language, "Kanata" meant village. Unlike her students, who could trace our ancestors to places outside the country's borders, she knew only one land.

It was the first time someone explained Canada was not just a place; Canada was also a time. It was impossible to draw a start date, showing when the land began. But the beginning of Canada was clear. It was the year someone from another place decided to give the land a new name.

She was my first Indigenous teacher, and the first Indigenous person I ever met. Before her, no one said there was a difference between people who were from Canada and people who were from somewhere else. Isolated in the affluent community twenty-five kilometres east of downtown Ottawa, I learned there were two main people in Canada: those who spoke English and those who spoke French. My community was unique; it was one of the few places in Ontario with many people who spoke French.

This was the first year we had a designated class for history. Madame Leclerc chopped up the text like an editor, striving to create the most accurate and interesting story, crossing out verbs in past tense and replacing them with the present tense. Indigenous peoples, she insisted, were not people who once lived, they were people who still existed—even if we did not see them. With the assistance of inserted photocopied pages from books we had never read, she recounted a story.

It was the late nineteenth century and European settlement was soaring. The government was pushing First Nations peoples into designated territories. The government called these areas reserves, land set aside for people who lived here before Canada. Then people came, she said, and took their children to *pensions*. A *pension* was a school only for Indigenous children. A place where lessons focused on rubbing out

Indigenous culture and replacing it with something British or French—
something *Canadian*. That way, the government could turn them into
'apples': red on the outside, white on the inside. The children were not
just taken, they were kidnapped.

Kidnapped to go to school? I thought. *Weird*. I wanted to ask why people
with brown skin were called red. I wanted to ask why First Nations children had to be forced to go to school and why they did not have their
own schools. I wanted to ask what was wrong with Indigenous culture,
why it needed to be changed. But Madame Leclerc was in the middle of
a lesson and was not to be interrupted.

She closed the book, loose papers still hanging out of the edges, and
laid it on her desk. I started to raise my hand when she walked back to
the front of the room. She pointed her index finger to the ceiling like a
preacher ready to start a sermon.

Her uncle grew up in a *pension*. Every time he tried to speak his language, teachers pierced the sides of his tongue. She stuck out her tongue
and pressed her fingers against it.

He never spoke his language again.

She looked at the floor, as if in search of something she would not
find. Her grandfather had suffered a stroke. Lying on his hospital bed,
he started speaking his language again. It was the first time she saw her
father cry. Within the walls of a government-sanctioned institution, they
had recovered something that was stolen from them.

Because of the treatment Indigenous children suffered at these *pensions*,
Madame Leclerc said, many returned home and could not transition back
into their families. Some never returned; others were ignored by their
communities. They were angry at their treatment. Some began drinking
alcohol to deal with their pain. When they were adults and had children
of their own, many copied their school treatment at home. For the first
time, she said, children in Indigenous families were beaten. Madame
Leclerc described this as a pattern, a pattern of abuse.

During quiet reading time, I was hunched over an open textbook like
all the other students. Madame Leclerc approached my seat. Her palm
squarely on the desk, time had etched stories into the creases of her

sixty-three-year-old skin. She leaned over and ran her finger under the words, "Many Indigenous children suffered at these *pensions*," underlining a meaning not evident. I cocked my left eyebrow and lifted my chin towards her. Her eyes were steady, her eyebrows slightly raised. I looked down at the page; I saw only black letters arranged neatly next to each other.

––––––––––

I knocked my elbow against the wall each time my arm drifted too far from the centre of the desk. Muscles in my hand ached from gripping the pen too tightly. Once again, I had done something to annoy my grade six teacher and once again I had found myself with an in-school suspension. It had only been fifteen minutes and I was already tired of completing the worksheet. It was mandatory to fill out a worksheet answering questions about the 'infraction' I had committed. In this case, it was defiance: the one word whose dictionary definition I had written so many times I could quote it without looking. Each time I was sent to her, the vice-principal shoved the same worksheet in my hands and escorted me to the Alternative Learning Centre, where all 'bad kids' served their in-school suspensions. A student on an in-school suspension was not an active participant at school. I was confined to that room all day, including recesses and lunch hour. I did not have access to any of the teacher's lessons from that day, so I tried to do what homework I could.

My cubicle was in the far corner of the room. The pencil markings I drew on the desk two weeks before were still there. Whenever the teacher demanded I do something without asking the same of other students and I disobeyed, she waltzed to the intercom in our classroom. She spoke loud enough for other students to hear and look up from their work, "I'm sending Miss Wright down to the office." I placed my pencil on the desk, pushed in the chair, and began the stroll to the front of the school. Looking down at the grey tiles, waxed that morning, I focused on my steps to avoid making eye contact with teachers in the classrooms I passed; they all knew where I was going.

Grade six was a bad year; the bullying got worse. I had become accustomed to jokes about my brown skin. "You look like a piece of poo," a red-headed girl once snapped back during an argument.

I was the only Black girl in the class, and my body became the most visible object in the room. I started puberty, and my mother bought me my first bra. My hips grew five inches, but I kept my ten-year-old waist. I had to buy pants that were a size five even though I was a size two, so there was enough space for my butt. It was my mother's idea to fasten the sides of my pants with safety pins; the pins kept fabric in place and were not damaged by the washing machine.

My body transformed into a touchable museum exhibit, where students explored their curiosities: How many pencils could they slide into my thick curls before I noticed? Why did my hair bounce back when they tugged on it? In gym class, I clenched the muscles in my butt whenever I was standing so that when students threw basketballs at it, they would not have the satisfaction of seeing it jiggle.

The teacher, a round woman with a pudgy face, stayed silent. I preferred her silence to the giggles she sometimes made under her breath. I was a 'bad kid' and found few allies. Every time I came back from the Alternative Learning Centre, I had to reintegrate into class. Students watched as I walked to my desk and slid into the chair. Like a prisoner returning at the end of a sentence.

One day I was sick and went to the nurse's office; my brother and I traded strep throat for almost a year until our doctor urged us to use different hand towels and toothpaste. That day, Madame Leclerc came to visit. I was in her last class before she retired and she sometimes visited her former students to say hello. My back hunched forward in the chair, a half-glass of flat ginger ale in my hand, when she walked in. She pulled up a chair, leaned back, and folded her arms. "So, how are things these days?" she said, her lips pursed as if she already knew the answer.

"Fine."

"Oh really?" She leaned forward so her eyes were directly in front of mine. I scrunched my hands under my chin, my elbows dug into the table. I stared into the ginger ale as the last bubble fizzed. "I hear you have been getting in trouble a lot."

I bit my bottom lip before I summoned up the courage to respond. "Yes."

She sighed. I expected her to give me a lecture about how important it was to listen to my teachers. "I know it is not easy. But you cannot learn if you are not in class. You are too smart to waste your time in that room." She got up from the chair and told me to keep studying hard.

I watched her walk out of the room. Barely taller than I was, her forceful demeanour garnered respect from students and teachers. A strict disciplinarian, she could silence any noisy room with a shout of a single word, "Three!" I could not understand why she was not upset.

———————

A law that was supposed to change everything. I looked at the cliché in the opening line and was convinced I would bomb the assignment. It had been a few years since the government enacted the Safe Schools Act, and my grade ten teacher demanded we learn about it. A very important law, she called it. I read through the opening passages and knew exactly what it was supposed to do: weed out the bad kids and suspend them. *Sure, that will make schools safe,* I thought, chuckling to myself. *Safe for who?*

I had another assignment on my mind: English. The teacher insisted we learn how to formulate an argument and deliver it in front of people. It would help us in our future lives, she said. Twirling her fingers through her long black hair, she instructed us to write a rant.

I sat on my bed with three pages torn out of the yellow notebook where I often wrote my thoughts; safe schools could wait. The blank pages sought the companionship of ink from the pen resting on the comforter. *What would people think if I did this?* But I knew it didn't matter. I was tired. Of the jokes, the insults, the stupid stereotypes that made no sense. I was angry and I wanted to prod them into anger too. I grabbed the pen and scratched the topic at the top of the page. The tip forced its way through the paper and onto the book I was using as a writing surface when I underlined the title: RACISM.

"There is no such thing as reverse racism," my hand scribbled in a fury of barely legible words. I wanted to attack the ridiculous response I often heard when I complained to teachers and friends about unfair treatment. I looked down at the two-page paragraph and scoffed, *this will really get them going.*

I stood at the front of the classroom, staring at students in the second row. I shifted between the page and my classmates as I spoke each line. My voice grew louder when I got to the part on reverse racism. A blonde-haired girl in the front row bit into her fingernails and peered at the floor. Perhaps she thought my presentation was payback for not skipping over the word *nigger* when it was her turn to read *To Kill a Mockingbird* aloud. When I finished my speech, students looked at each other, not knowing whether it was okay to clap. I walked to my seat, my chin parallel to the floor, and leaned back into the chair. I didn't look towards the teacher's desk; her opinion didn't matter. She told us to write a rant, so I ranted.

We got our results. I got an A and a simple comment:

Great passion.

Apparently, I was good at being angry.

———

"Angela," the teacher called across the silent classroom, "the principal wants to see you."

Snickers rose from chairs behind me. I knew exactly what she wanted to discuss. I tossed my textbook, notebook, and calculator in my backpack and headed to the office.

It was only two months until graduation, but she wasn't going to make this easy. When I walked into her office, Ben was already sitting there. His dirty blonde hair peeked under the red baseball cap he always wore; as though toques weren't readily available in Canada during the winter months. He looked at me as I sat down, smirking.

The principal swivelled in her chair and leaned in towards us. "Ben tells me you had an argument and said some nasty things to him on the bus this morning," she said.

"Yes, I told him to shut the fuck up."

Her eyes widened as though she had seen a ghost. "Why?"

"Because I'm so tired." I let out a huge sigh, and my shoulders dropped into the back of the chair. "I don't care about him." I folded my arms and sank my hands under my armpits. "He hangs out with those white supremacists and I know what they say about Black people, they've been bothering us all—"

"But I know what it's like to be discriminated against," Ben interjected. "I'm Italian and kids used to make fun of me because I had curly hair."

The principal stuck her hand in front of his face and he recoiled into his chair. "That is not quite the same thing. It is important to understand that slurs used to insult Black people are not the same as being made fun of because you have curly hair," she said.

I looked at her and blinked four times before I realized she was serious. It was the first time she had shown any concern for Black students. When a white student who was part of the crew of white supremacists on campus showed up to a dance with *SKIN HEAD* emblazoned on his shirt, she was unfazed by his drunken threats to go after Black students.

My thoughts filled the void of silence as I remembered every slight from the past year. The many times a white supremacist bumped me while I was reaching into my locker, each time white supremacists used the word "nic-nack," like we didn't know it was a stand-in for *nigger*. The wad of spit that flew out of a white supremacist's mouth and landed on my friend's cheek. I closed my eyes to prevent tears from forming. When I opened my eyes, all the frustrations converged on the tip of my tongue and I blurted out, "You don't know how hard it is to be a minority. We get so little supp—"

"What do you mean? Black people are not minorities," the principal said. "There are plenty of Black people at this school. The real problem is that you self-segregate yourselves."

My shoulders fell forward, and I clasped my hands between my thighs. There was so much to say, but it was pointless. I knew the name of every Black student in that high school. I made a list in the fall when I was trying to solicit support for Black History Month. Out of one thousand students, twenty were Black; twenty too many, apparently.

I saw her lips move, but didn't hear anything. It was time for me to go. The matter was settled; she wasn't going to discipline me for cursing on a school bus.

I threw my backpack onto my shoulders and walked out of the office. I turned to walk to the classroom, but went outside instead. The breeze brushed against my face and I felt the weight of the textbook on my shoulders. I sat on the ledge; my back couldn't stay straight and I slouched forward, elbows on my knees. Looking at the ground, I thought about Madame Leclerc. I wondered if she still returned to school to visit even though all her former students were gone. Did she walk through the hallways, remembering the stories that were imprinted into the crinkles in her skin? Did her children ever learn her native language? I looked out at the parking lot, hoping I would see her striding towards the building. I wanted her to sit on the stone ledge next to me. To lean forward with her eyes directly in front of mine and tell me, tell me she understood.

SHAME AND
THE KINSHIP OF
SEXUAL VIOLENCE

— RACHEL ZELLERS —

All community accountability work is science fiction, because it calls
us to create that which has never been created. At least, not yet.
—Inspired by Octavia's Brood

My mother was raped for the first time when she was a teenager. My mother, a small-town girl from central Pennsylvania, was sodomized by a local college boy one night during a campus party. When she told me this story, she recalled that her body had been pressed into saliva-moistened leather seats of a red convertible my grandparents could never have afforded. There was another rape and more sexual violence during her heavy drug-using years before she got clean, but it was this experience of being a young woman—drunk, aroused, deeply curious, and losing her body for the first time—that she wanted me to know about first. I was fifteen or sixteen when she first shared this history with me.

I don't know exactly what I did with that story of my mother's rape through my college years. I fucked. Made love. Had unprotected sex.

Watched friends turn up HIV positive. I was sexually assaulted in college, and when I graduated it is fair to say that my relationship with my body was still an ambiguous one regarding the full safety of it. My mother's story, as I understand now, was only intended, in part, as warning. The information she intended to impart pertains to shame and the familial kinship of sexual violence.

It has taken the last twenty-five years to experience the full weight of my mother's story of rape. I spent my teenage years in Narcotics Anonymous (NA) meetings in West Baltimore with my mom, where she spoke openly in front of me and a room full of strangers about her past and her feelings of shame as part of her recovery. She was full of shame for what she had done to friends and family members during her active addiction years. Before she went into rehab for the first time, a month or two before she nearly overdosed, she left my three-year-old brother with a man she had known for only a few weeks while she was working the night shift. He sexually assaulted my baby brother and altered the course of his life forever. My mother went into rehab soon after she chased this man out of our apartment with a baseball bat. I had just departed for my father's house for the summer. I don't exactly know what the outcome of that attack was; it occurs to me only now that perhaps her first trip to rehab was a way of avoiding charges or jail time for assault. And maybe this explains why she relapsed so easily the first time, too. I do know that she lost her nursing license, and so, lost her only means to provide a decent life for me and my baby brother. My brother and I lived with our fathers, two different men, for the next few years.

Our absences only increased my mother's shame. When my father found out that my mother was in rehab, my annual month-long summer trip turned into two years in his house. Certainly, my mother knew what kind of violence I would witness in my father's care. Certainly, she suspected what kind of damage would be done, and she suffered knowing that she was powerless over it. As a mother now, I cannot imagine what it took her to trust that I would somehow be all right while we were separated for those two years. I used to think that I would have died.

But now I understand the greater terror in leaving behind children without me alive to fight for them. I would indeed survive, and she must have believed that too. My mother relapsed only once.

My mother was ashamed, too, that she had had so much sex in ways that she had not enjoyed and that, in the process, she had caused great harm to her body. She was ashamed of the way my grandfather had put his hands on her when he first recognized desire in her. I can remember how my mother cried when she first shared with me the beating my grandfather had given her in tenth grade for coming home on a Friday night with a passion mark on her neck. She had bounded through the door at curfew, she explained, excited, joyful, and filled with a quiet pleasure she held from making out with a boy who had been tender with her. This boy had made her body feel good and safe, and he had respected her boundaries while they stood together, hands and mouths wandering, making out behind her high school building. She had no idea he had given her a hickey, but my grandfather saw it immediately when she came in the door, giddy, with her best friend trailing behind. Before she could form a full sentence of explanation—her pleasure, please, no sex in it—my grandfather snapped his leather belt loose from his waist and came down upon her body. As she told me this story, she recalled all the places he beat her that night: the hunched length of her long spine, her forearms, flailing hands and fingertips, calves, and the fronts of her legs, as she stood spinning wildly and partially disrobed, in the centre of my grandparent's living room. "I always remember that beating against the pleasure I felt coming in the door," she said as she finished telling me the story. My mother also had her period that night.

Afterwards, she explained, shame and pleasure and the safety of her body got all jumbled up in her mind. She was ashamed of the things that were good for her, ashamed that she had wounded her father somehow, ashamed because his eyes averted away from hers for years after that beating. "I felt a shame that I had never known possible before that night; I still feel it," she shared with me. My mother also told me this story when I was fifteen or sixteen, and when she was done, she promised to never shame me for my sexual desires or my sexual explorations.

She honoured that promise in full through my high school and college years until she died in 1999.

I think of her feelings of shame a lot because she so desperately did not want me to carry it on my body, as she had grafted it onto hers. She spoke of this often. My mother was beautiful, kind, graceful and yet, as her daughter, I could always feel the facade of this disposition. As her daughter, I felt a woman who was waiting for the love of her life to return to her from Vietnam (a sweet, devoted man named Greg); a woman who settled for very little in a man the first time cancer besieged her body; and then finally, a woman who let the dream of romantic love go with the opportunity to live a bit longer. She stayed single through her second bout of cancer, when her body finally buckled under the weight of its metastasized vigour and its reminder of the liver she had destroyed when she was shooting drugs regularly into her veins. The shame that she carried with her to the very end of her life, that she expressed in her fears and simple, abundant gratitudes in the last few days of her life, was two-fold: she was deeply ashamed that she had failed to protect my baby brother—then fifteen and raging beyond her control—and she was ashamed of all the war she had waged upon her body.

As my mother lay dying in her bed, I shared with her how grateful I was that she had protected me as a child and as a young woman. I was grateful she had fought her way back to me after she came out of rehab, that we had a full decade together before she died from cancer. I was grateful—so very grateful—that she had never left me alone with strange men during our years together or placed any partner, any love, or any lover before me. As a child, I would regularly tiptoe into her room in the middle of the night to sleep next to her, and my space next to her body was never filled. She kept an intentional distance between our home and her lovers, and she never let other men parent or discipline me. Our home was never a resting place for new men, abusive men, and I can recall only one or two times during my high school years when a lover joined us for dinner or a family outing. I was grateful, also, that she never disappeared again or left me to care for my younger brother, eight years my junior. Those choices of distance and solitude that my mother made saved my life.

And these choices, I believe, are the thing that keeps me so tethered to my own three young children. Her choices have helped me lean into my aloneness as a place of solitude rather than absence and find comfort in this place.

In her expressions of shame, I know that my mother was testing the boundaries of her own loveableness with me. To see whether or not her own daughter could unconditionally love a mother who had positioned her children within spaces of so much violence. To see whether or not I could love a woman who had been raped more than once in the process of looking for something better than herself. I know she wondered, at times, whether she deserved to be loved at all. I also know now that the feelings that flooded me in the moments before and after my mother died were feelings of the highest kind of love for this woman who had bared herself raw to me, who had extended her heart to me when my teenage rage was most palpable, and who had dared to ask for forgiveness for things that I still cannot write about.

I mean in no way to cast my mother as a saint. I am both clear and comfortable that she was not. I have reflected about my mother and our relationship a great deal over the last five years while organizing my work against sexual violence. Specifically, I have reflected upon what draws human beings towards the work of accountability in the context of sexual violence, and also what causes people to fall away to the margins as silent supporters, the ambiguous or the outright opposed. In my first year of work, I attempted my first accountability process with a well-known, local community organizer. When his close friend, an academic and labour organizer of colour, heard about the process, he sent a message to me through a mutual friend: "Fuck community accountability."

What kind of self-reckoning is demanded for anti-violence work and community accountability? And, most importantly, what kind of relationship with our own bodies do we need in order to accept accountability work involving sexual violence? Community accountability is work that bears no template, no ending point, no certainty, and yet, calls us into its centre to face violence again and again. What happens to a body that cannot bear this violence or retreats to a distant place as a result of this work? Can we train ourselves to swim towards or away from the epicentre when we need to?

I share this story of my mother and the histories of violence running between us for a few reasons. I believe that she would allow me to share it.

First, I don't believe that any useful organizing or activism—particularly in the context of Black women and our experiences of violence—can escape our personal introspection, a return to our childhoods, or our own histories of violence. It is something I am still learning to fully articulate, but I am certain of the destructive disjuncture between the 'personal and political' (or in academia, 'the personal and theoretical') I witness all around me. Continually, I witness human beings who have razor-sharp analyses and discourses—professors and academics, student activists, community organizers—but treat their children and lovers and kin with a violence that makes my heart hurt. Long-time community organizer adrienne maree brown has asked this question, "How do we say, 'let's make justice the most pleasurable experience a human can involve themselves in?'" Regardless of the limitations of "justice," I hear an urgency to deepen the love and integrity in our most personal relationships so that this sensuality and care seeps into all of the work that we do.

Secondly, I talk about my mother often because the silence in our families, in our communities, and in Black women's relationships regarding our histories of violence is still deafening. And this silence is, quite literally, killing us. The silence is making us unwell, stealing away our capacities for expanding into our most glorious, unbound selves as we age. This process of 'killing' has a long genealogy bound up in our Black radical traditions. I am only now, in my mid-forties, learning how to speak in any detail about the histories of sexual and partnership violence in my own family and life. There are many levels of violence in my family tree, and I am committed to learning how to reckon with the most difficult instances. More challenging is the process of getting clearer about how these family histories have impacted me and bleed into my present life and relationships with people I love.

One of the mental mistakes I made beginning this work was believing that my life would somehow become easier—that I would somehow experience less violence and pain around me if I was organizing against sexual violence. I was very wrong. What I instead found was a pain that increased and knocked against my threshold. I realize now that pain will always return, that this work brings the violence of my past into my chest like a fountain recycling its water, and that the only way to thrive in relation to this work is to allow the pain in, until it becomes like water washing over me. Allowing this, however, requires deepening my threshold for love and joy and touch and pleasure in other areas of my life simultaneously.

Finally, I also share this story about my mother because I believe that our personal histories of violence inscribe a trajectory in our lives that determines how we deal with violence when it hits home again. And violence always returns to the places where we believe we are finally safe again. The failure to face the hot pain of our personal histories of violence compounds with age. How do we fail the people closest to us when we cannot—and do not—do right by women in our community who have experienced sexual violence? I am constantly guided by this question: What kind of tools am I leaving behind for my three children?

My mother insisted on sharing her histories of violence with me. She was committed to not shame me as a sexually active young woman. In confronting and sharing the shame wielded upon her by her own father, she granted me freedom, joy, and the permission to explore sexually the first time I fell in love at sixteen. This is the same freedom I hope to pass on to my own children.

AS LONG AS THEY THINK THEY ARE WHITE

— *Scott Fraser* —

My father immigrated to Canada from Jamaica as a child. Ours was one of the first Caribbean families to arrive after Canada changed its racist immigration policies in 1962. With a great deal of ability, tenacity, and luck my grandfather was able to establish himself as a lawyer, first in Toronto, then Kingston, and eventually in Ottawa. His efforts and good fortune paved the way for my father's generation to go to university and become established middle-class professionals. The socio-economic success of my Jamaican family reinforced our conservatism. Canada, despite lingering elements of racism, was a place with limitless possibilities so long as one was willing to work hard. Protest was something that happened in places without possibilities. I learned about the Civil Rights movements in the United States, I learned about resistance to slavery, and the efforts to integrate North American society. But race was more or less presented to me as something that had been largely solved. Therefore contemporary protestors were dismissed as layabouts, professional malcontents, and rabble-rousers.

I abandoned the right-wing politics I'd grown up with by my early twenties, politically hovering somewhere between the Liberal and New Democratic parties, but nevertheless I generally shared the inherited view that protest belonged to a past era and that everything would be fine with an occasional and minor adjustment here and there.

One of the turning points for me was the government's heavy-handed reaction during the G20 Summit in Toronto. I'd actually been involved in planning the military's involvement in that operation as a commissioned army officer on the Area Command staff. It was my insistence (largely ignored) that my fellow officers stop thinking of civilian protestors as enemy forces that made me start to lose confidence in the ability of state institutions to respond rationally to calls to adjust the status quo. I saw racist attitudes concerning the surveillance of Indigenous groups, also regarded as enemy forces, rather than as First Peoples making perfectly legitimate demands to adjust the status quo. I'd left the army by the time the summit took place. I hadn't joined any radical groups or anything like that, but I saw my city transformed into a fortress in order to protect state leaders who really, in my liberal view, ought not to have had anything to fear from the public they supposedly served. I rode my bike out to observe some of the protests and witnessed the crackdown that took place outside the temporary holding cells on Eastern Avenue. The images stuck with me.

Then came Occupy Wall Street. Again, I saw state institutions that were completely incapable of responding rationally to legitimate grievances. I spent some time at the encampment in Toronto. The movement sparked my interest in more radical thought, and while to this day I'm not a part of any particular organization or movement, I'm a fellow traveller and the lens through which I observe society was forever altered.

In the years following Occupy, I've watched several mass mobilizations ebb and flow. The one I'd like to speak to is Black Lives Matter Toronto (BLMTO).

My successful immigrant family had constructed an image of Canada being a place that had largely solved its race problem, but the gilded facade hid a rotten structure. As soon as one looks past the lives of the small but highly visible Black bourgeoisie, one can't help but see the dire necessity for a revolution in our understanding of the race question in Canada. This is why I've become a critical supporter of Black Lives Matter in Canada.

Some of the movement's most prominent members (notably Yusra Kogali) have said some profoundly outlandish things about race, including:

"Whiteness is not humxness."

"In fact white skin is subhumxn."

"White people are recessive genetic defects. This is factual."

But I'd rather call her in than call her out. She clearly doesn't understand the science of genetics and evolutionary biology, but she's also hardly the first Black radical to go down the road of reversing European race theory. These ideas aren't a new phenomenon in radical Black circles. Elijah Muhammed and the Nation of Islam embraced a similar set of hierarchical racial theories that placed Blacks at the top. Whites, to Muhammed, weren't even human. At least, they weren't creations of Allah. They were devils. Muhammed and his more famous protégé, Malcolm X, did much for Black people in North America, but their ideas about race (which Malcolm would later reject) need to be dismissed out of hand. They are informed by the same kind of pseudoscience that inspired some of the worst moral catastrophes in the history of our species. African exceptionalism must be rejected alongside eugenics, Nazism, slavery, white supremacy, and American exceptionalism.

Nothing good comes from travelling those worn-out roads.

That said, I support the spirit of BLM even though I've come to the somewhat paradoxical conclusion that it has reached its limits as a movement and will never be able to achieve the revolutionary objective on its own. BLM has had success in various locations at adjusting this or that policy on police profiling, or drawing attention to specific cases of police brutality, and so on. But as currently constructed, it's not a revolutionary movement.

I've said that we need a revolution in race. So why would I claim that BLM (which I love and respect) has reached its limits? The answer has to do with the nature of the problem. The race question in Canada and other comparable societies has to do with the notion of Whiteness.

The required revolution, in a real sense, has nothing to do with us Africans living in Canada. It's not our problem.

All we can do is try to live our lives as if we had a right to exist and, by so doing, hold up a mirror to the Europeans we live amongst. Our protest movements have value to that end, but the revolution in race needs to occur within self-identified white people. Let us, to quote James Baldwin, return to them their problem. Because as long as they think they're white, there's no hope for them.

JAMES BALDWIN'S INSIGHT

Baldwin's formula, which I've borrowed, might hit the ears of self-described white people as sharply as the remarks Yusra made, so it requires explanation. The key distinction is, whereas Yusra claims a defect in whites, I claim instead that there is a defect in Whiteness.

'Whiteness' was invented to separate. It holds no explanatory value. Its margins are arbitrary and shifting. As Africans, we really shouldn't believe in race. Science doesn't support the notion. Race is a story that has been told to convince some people that it's okay to dominate or destroy other people. We can do without it. At least I can. We Africans can contribute to a race revolution simply by rejecting European notions of race. Living as if we had a right to exist is an act of revolution.

Why is it so hard for white people to let go of the stories they've invented? There is no such thing as a white human or a black human. These are divisions that are experienced socially and politically, but there is no substantive, material difference between us. White and Black? These are categories invented and utilized by Europeans to act as a kind of psychological balm. Perhaps to sooth guilty consciences as Europeans set out to dominate and control other populations. It was okay to enslave, to colonize, to eradicate, to segregate, to imprison, to hate, to lynch because there was something about Whiteness that had to be protected. On some level, likely a subconscious one, even the most radical and/or progressive 'white' person shares the same racial ideology as the worst Klansman or Nazi, otherwise they wouldn't be categorizing us as Black and themselves as white. They could instead call themselves what they are, European (settlers).

Baldwin's brilliant psychological insight was to point out that what one says about others reveals more about the speaker than their subject. In other words, when white people invented the racial categories we live with today, it revealed something about them. When white people today maintain the categories their ancestors created, it reveals something about them...not us.

Baldwin put it more forcefully when he said of white people, "You're the nigger baby, it isn't me." The philosopher Cornel West defines niggerization as the process of being made to feel so scared, insecure, and intimidated that you defer to the powers that be, that you consent to your own domination. So in this Trump moment, and with the rise in North America of vicious, murderous alt-right racists, I ask, who's the nigger? The Black people straightening their backs up and living as if they have a right to exist? Or the European people collectively losing their minds over perceived threats to their stories about Whiteness? Baldwin knew that the nigger (or the Negro, or the coloured, or the Black) was an invention of the white man and was a reflection of his fear, insecurity, and uncertainty. We didn't need race, but they sure seemed to. The nomenclature changes, but the categories do not. This, incidentally, is why politically correct language does nothing to stop racism or any other form of oppressive hate. White people can call me nigger or they can call me Black, but no matter how rude or polite their words, the categories belong to them. Who's in, who's out. It's decided by their gaze and on their terms.

So what do we call ourselves? Who are we? Where are we from?

"Where are you from?"

I am asked this question often. And it takes on a different meaning depending on who is asking. When I hear it from another Black or brown person, I generally take it as an attempt to find out whether we share some kind of geography. Are we both Jamaican? Might we both have roots in the islands? Might I be a fellow Indian or Arab? But the question feels different when posed by someone who presents as white.

When white folks ask me where I'm from and I say that I was born in Ottawa and have lived primarily in the Greater Toronto Area, they find my answer unsatisfactory. They were 'politely' asking about my skin, not my birth certificate or where I went to school. The truthful answer, and one that I hope can be used by everybody who is interested in starting to abolish the racial categories invented by white people, is that I'm of mixed European and African descent, but as long as Whiteness exists, I know precisely that I am a Black man. I'm not 'biracial'. In fact, the now offensive term 'mulatto' is far more honest than 'biracial,' since we would never apply the terms 'mixed' or 'biracial' to the product of an Anglo-German coupling, or the child of a Norwegian and a Dutch couple. In the context of a politely white supremacist society like Canada, terms like biracial and Black are merely the politically correct forms of mulatto and nigger.

For us African people in Canada, 'Black' is at once a term of pride and a term of erasure, depending on the context. Amongst ourselves, and I think we intuitively know who we are on some level, 'Black' can bring us together in the best tradition of Pan-Africanism. We know it when we show extra concern for each other in predominantly white spaces. We know it by the way we can breathe just a little bit easier when we're not alone in this society that doubts our desirability. We know it because it's understood that we vouch for the Europeans we introduce into our circles. "This one's alright," may not be spoken, but I suspect it's widely understood. We know it when a white friend notices that we acknowledge each other just because of the love we have for who we are. In racially mixed circles it's sometimes called "the Black nod." This kind of solidarity is important and beautiful and must be expanded as a matter of survival.

But the flip side is that we live in a white supremacist world. That world erases the fact that we've come from so many different places and over so many generations that we all have our own geography and history. Some of us are descended from slaves. Our previous geography is mostly unknown, but we proudly claim beautiful islands in the Caribbean, or the vibrant communities former slaves built in Nova Scotia and Ontario.

Others have come more recently from Africa, and in that case may find it perplexing to be lumped under the umbrella 'Black' when, until they arrived here, they were Somali, Amhara, Zulu, Igbo, or any of the hundreds of other distinct cultures that call Africa home. Welcome to Canada, my brothers and sisters. Here you're reduced to your colour, and nothing about where you came from will protect you from the assumptions and the violence of a European settler project built on white supremacy.

Before we were niggers, negroes, coloureds, and Blacks, we Africans born of the West had a geography. We had our own peoples and places. I reject romantic notions of pre-contact Africa, but good, bad, and ugly, it was ours. The slave trade ended that geography for my family and we became niggers, negroes, coloureds, mulattoes, and now Blacks and biracials. White supremacy erases the more recent African arrivals, shoe-horning anyone with dark skin into categories invented by Europeans. To the European eye, it doesn't matter if we're descended from the families of Africville, Nova Scotia, Jamaican slaves, or recent Somali immigrants. They just see Blacks.

But let's agree to a basic level of honesty. I'm here as the son of enslaved Africans brought to the colony of Jamaica. Much like Canada, Jamaica was built on the European destruction of Indigenous people. We migrated to the settler-colonial project known as Canada essentially as economic refugees. Refugees from a system that compensated our former masters for the loss of their property (our bodies, brains, and labour) while imposing on us an economic system that kept and continues to keep us poor and hungry, with limited opportunity to flourish. Eventually Canada's appetite for cheap labour encouraged a 'liberalizing' of its immigration policy, allowing us Blacks to come in numbers dwarfing those of the much celebrated Underground Railroad, only to be denied the same opportunities white people can so often take for granted.

The same white people who applaud the Underground Railroad from the safe distance of the centuries don't do a damn thing today to prevent the hyper-exploitation of Black and brown 'temporary foreign workers'. They don't say a mumbling word about police violence, mass incarceration, and the myriad of other examples of institutionalized racism in this country. And mostly, they don't do a damn thing to challenge or begin to dismantle the racial categories their ancestors invented and they maintain. The needed revolution begins there. We have our role to play, including in our protest, but I want to stress that it's not our task to dismantle Whiteness.

This isn't a cheap rhetorical game. How we think of others, as Baldwin pointed out, says more about ourselves than it does the subjects of our thought and speech. So it matters how we think and verbalize the experience of race (built as it is on unscientific nonsense). This work, I claim, is up to self-identified white people. They can continue to maintain their racial categories or they can start to dismantle them. Only one course of action will make them my brother, sister, or comrade.

I'm very glad that Black Lives Matter Toronto exists.

I think their greatest achievement isn't the pressure they've put on various governments to end this or that racist policy. It isn't calling attention to the extrajudicial murders of African people by the police. The greatest success of the movement both here and around North America is that it has, for the first time since the heydays of the Nation of Islam and the Black Panther Party, put so-called white people on notice. BLM scares white people. And considering that local BLM movements have not gone beyond the most peaceful and moderate of tactics, this is telling. BLM isn't a revolutionary movement and it still upsets and terrifies Europeans, some of whom have taken to postering our streets with dog-whistle messages declaring that "It's Okay To Be White."

It used to take armed militants like the Panthers and the Nation to shock whites into seeing the pain and suffering of Black people living in their midst. Now all it takes is a highway sit-in or a minor delay in a corporatized Pride parade to cause great wailing and gnashing of teeth among white people. Hopefully those Europeans living in North America will begin to address their race problem before, to end on another Baldwin quote, "the fire next time."

A FAMILY COMPLICATION

WRITING ABOUT RACE AS A BLACK, SOUTH ASIAN WOMAN

— *ETERNITY MARTIS* —

"So what do you think about Black Lives Matter hijacking the Pride parade?"

It took me by surprise. I was talking about my journalism career, which is mainly composed of race and gender issues, when this statement, disguised as an innocent question, shot out into the air, wounding me with the same dangerous language that I reserved for far-right and conservative white folks. Except, it came from the mouth of a family member.

It was an action I had spent the summer vigorously defending in my work and social interactions. And it was an emotional issue I felt invested in at a time when people were becoming increasingly vocal about race relations in Canada. Now, I was trying to defend this against a blood relative who used to play with me as a baby.

I am an anomaly in my family. I'm an only child, born out of wedlock to a single Pakistani mother and an absent Jamaican father, raised in a loving South Asian family.

Though I resemble my mother and grandmother, I have Black Caribbean features; while they spend hundreds of dollars perming their hair, mine is naturally thick and curly. They were so confused by its unruliness that all they could do was compress it into braids saturated with Dippity Doo and Infusium 23 detangler. For almost twenty years, I was the only Black biracial person in my family.

High school was a time when I realized that being biracial was incredibly complicated. I had trouble making Black or South Asian friends, both too puzzled by my ethnicities to know how to approach me. It was then that I noticed I looked different from the rest of my family, much to the surprise of my mother and grandfather, who were oblivious to the stark difference in our physical traits. The rest of my family never seemed to notice my difference either.

However, the way I was perceived and subsequently treated by strangers reeked of anti-black racism, which became more evident when I moved to the predominantly white city of London, Ontario, to attend Western University at the age of eighteen. The impact of anti-black racism—and racism in general—from individuals and societal structures was so profound for me and my identity, a sheltered girl from the multicultural city of Toronto, that I dedicated all my academic papers, then my writing, then my journalism career, to unearthing race relations.

But writing about anti-black racism baffled my South Asian family. Anti-black racism, police brutality, carding, Black history in Canada—all the things I wrote and cared about were never brought up in conversation. For a while I misread their silence as acceptance of the subjects I covered; but instead, they were confused. Finally, at a party, I got the answer I feared.

"But you're not one of them," a distant cousin once scoffed. "You're one of us."

It wouldn't be the first time I heard this, but it didn't make it any easier to understand. My existence is bound to a group they turn up their noses at. It suggests that I shouldn't worry; that one part of me is still morally superior, even though the other part may be inherently degenerate. Though it took several years for my immediate family to finally understand how my experience differs from theirs, my extended family still cannot understand that I share very different experiences than their own. I cannot be one of them when I am constantly asked if I (the friend) need a separate bill when we're out for dinner. Not when we travel to Karachi and family friends think I'm adopted. Nor when I am doubled over in agony each month by endometriosis, a condition that overwhelmingly affects Black women. Or when white men tell me I'm cute for a Black girl, or call me a nigger. Explaining this is exhausting and fruitless. They don't get that I am not them, but by nature something quite different.

Mixed-race people are one of Canada's fastest growing demographics, with more than 360,000 mixed-race couples reported by Statistics Canada in 2011, more than double the total from twenty years ago. Though Canada is a multicultural country, things get messy when sex, love, marriage, or children are involved. For bi- or multiracial people, having the support of your family about the racism you experience is a complicated situation, especially when one side is not just considered a visible minority group, but defamed by social and historical stereotypes. You may feel the love of a family who shares one part of your heritage, but you also may feel their hatred or disdain for the other ethnicity within your DNA. Time and again, the parents of bi- and multiracial children face difficulty and tension when trying to understand their offsprings' differing experiences.

For my family, namely my extended family, the tension is not in the way I identify, but in the subjects I choose to write about. However, I don't think some members of my extended family are intentionally malicious, because they are quite taken aback when I call out their problematic behaviour or launch into a verbal essay refuting their beliefs. But part of being a more supportive loved one is knowing when your assumptions are out of whack. In my case, it's getting my family to realize that I don't experience the same discrimination they did when they first arrived in Canada in the 1970s, but a very different kind of oppression as a result of belonging to a second marginalized group—and that writing about anti-black racism doesn't mean I'm choosing a side or turning my back on the family I grew up in.

Anti-black racism in South Asian communities is alarming, but rarely outwardly discussed. Though a minority group, they are often considered superior to Black people's status, skin colour, and morality, which they then use against Black groups. Some use the derogatory term *kala* to refer to Black people, and harass, physically attack, and discriminate against them when they visit South Asian countries (a Nigerian master's student experienced heartbreaking racism while studying in Noida, New Delhi, and African students have been physically attacked in south Delhi). Indigenous African populations in India and Pakistan who have been there for centuries—Siddis and Sheedis—are pushed to the margins of society, often living in poverty, never given the chance to be a part of the larger community.

It's a shocking revelation, considering South Asian and Black people have worked together in the battle for freedom for decades, especially through writing. When the mainstream American newspapers presented stories about civil disobedience during India's fight for independence in 1942, the Black press covered the independence movements as resistance movements and Black activists supported the country's independence. It was the United States Civil Rights movement of action, activism, and words that helped secure the rights and freedoms that South Asian people were also able to enjoy, and in Canada both groups struggled against the words printed in Canada's immigration policy that caused obstacles to immigrating to the country.

Younger South Asians continue to come out and condemn anti-black racism in their communities through writing, including Arti Patel, a Toronto-based journalist, who wrote a piece for Huffington Post Canada called "South Asians really need to stop saying the n-word." Patel says she's lost track of the number of times she has observed South Asian people using the term. "South Asians can agree how anti-black many other South Asians in our communities and families can be," she writes. "Continuing to use this word—even if you're not doing it in a racist way—makes it seem like we've moved beyond the issue. We haven't."

Following the criticism after Black Lives Matter Toronto staged a sit-in during Pride 2016 until nine demands were met (which included support for Black and South Asian groups at Pride), Asian Canadians launched a letter-writing campaign to address anti-black racism in their communities and families. The letter, translated into over a dozen languages, details the unique experiences with discrimination, slavery, and racism that Black people face, and how they have helped secure rights for Asian Canadians. "Part of that means speaking up when I see people in my community—or my own family—say or do things that diminish the humanity of Black people," part of the letter reads. "I am telling you out of love, because I don't want this issue to divide us."

Writing that is honest and powerful is needed, now more than ever, given the current state of anti-black racism in Canada. It has the power to expose the truth, help people understand, and learn a little about the lives of people unlike them. At a time where our rights are being restricted and we are wholly changed by violence and discrimination, sharing our stories and the experiences of others is fundamental, as is calling out other racialized, oppressed groups for internalizing and using Whiteness against one another—even when it's by our loved ones.

Family never equates to immediate allyship, and no biracial child can fix decades of a loved one's uncorrected bias.

And it's not our job. Our Canadian multicultural landscape likens bi- and multiracial children to the future; it romanticizes us—our beauty, our mystery, our possibility—without acknowledging our struggles. While our physical presence can make our families and societies re-evaluate their views, it is ultimately up to them to actively confront themselves.

I won't stop writing about anti-black racism, but I also won't stop sharing it with my South Asian family. As a Black biracial woman, I not only use writing to teach and inform my family of the horrors of anti-black racism that the mainstream media often ignores, but it's a way for them to learn more about me and how I fit into the world. In the several years that I have been writing about race, my immediate family has started to engage in the conversations I write about, paying more attention to anti-black racism, acknowledging that I also identify as Black, supporting me, and feeling my fear and rage when I encounter racism. They know that we are not unchained from the same bloodline because I experience the world differently. They're starting to accept that not writing about South Asian issues doesn't mean I don't appreciate where I'm from. With some persistence and patience, I hope other members of my family will understand that their love for me also must include playing an active role in erasing racism, even if it means confronting themselves.

A funny thing happened not very long ago. At a dinner party, I was talking about my journalism career with a cousin, when the words shot out into the air: "So what do you think about Black Lives Matter hijacking the Pride parade?"

So I told him what I thought—the problematic language used by media, the reason for the sit-in, the things he didn't know from reading the paper, why I was in defense of their tactics. He knew none of it. After an apology to me, he wanted to know more. And then more about everything I write about. At that same table, a family member interrupted by saying that I wasn't one of "them," so she didn't get why I was always writing about Black issues. I tried to explain how my identity was tied to Blackness. She kept at it.

In a moment I wasn't expecting, my cousin put out his hand towards me, his voice silencing the growing, bitter tension, just in time, before embarrassing tears fell from my eyes. "Your experiences are your own, and you identify how you want to," he said. "You be who you are."

It was a small gesture that caused a mountain of relief. The next day, my Pakistani cousin sent me an email.

He asked if I could send him more of my work.

MY ANCESTORS' WILDEST DREAMS

INTERVIEWS OF IDENTITY, SELFHOOD, AND JOY WITH AFRO-INDIGENOUS YOUTH

The following is a compilation of interviews via email and phone correspondence conducted roundtable-style with four young people: Shammy Belmore, Simone Blais, Wenzdae Brewster, and Kaya Joan. Too often the experiences of folks with both African and Indigenous ancestry are omitted from the conversation about Black Canadian experience. This conversation seeks to centre these voices amidst Canada celebrating 150 years of Confederation, amidst anti-Indigenous sentiment throughout the country, amidst the tragedy of all Missing and Murdered Indigenous women, girls, and two-spirit people, amidst the verdicts of the Boushie and Fontaine cases. Acknowledgement, solidarity, and joy are in short supply.

Please describe your location in as much detail as you are comfortable with. This can be your physical location on Turtle Island, your ethnic

and cultural location, as well as your political location and other ways you wish to identify yourself.

Shammy: For me physically, I am located in Alberta, the capital city, a fast-paced place. I am located culturally within the First Nations community here in Edmonton and I am ethnically Somali. They both play a big role in my life. I have lived here forever. I haven't lived anywhere else.

I'm also located within the Edmonton artist community. I identify as a gender non-binary person within the queer community. I do not have a terribly strong political stance, although Alberta is more to the left.

Simone: I am a young, queer, brown woman. My dad is from Trinidad and my mom is Métis, born in Winnipeg. I was raised in downtown Toronto, which shaped my ability to see different cultures as normal. Growing up, my friends were Jamaican, Jewish, Chilean, Polish, Chinese, so I've always valued where I grew up. For the past four years, I've been living on Vancouver Island in Lekwungen and W̱SÁNEĆ territories. I'm a doula, a dancer, a writer, and a student.

Wenzdae: I am a city kid born of the Original Peoples of the Americas and the slaves brought on ships to die. I am a walking rebellion.

Kaya: I position myself differently depending on the day—and I am not always in control of everywhere I am existing. I find myself clocking my location constantly. Where is my mind? Where are my feet? Who walked before me here, and who will walk here after me? I feel myself lost in this colonial, imperial, patriarchal, suffocating mess. I ground myself by reminding my feet they are on Turtle Island, Tkaronto, Dish With One Spoon treaty territory. I feel far away from this land sometimes when I see only concrete around me. More and more I have been noticing all the old, beautiful trees in this city, which relocate my mind to a good place. I am a femme, a radical maker, and an empath. I am a cedar sapling, my roots running deep, stretching far and wide, my branches hungry for growth, always.

What are some moments when people challenge your lived experience, and what do you do to maintain those relationships?

Shammy: Immediately when I hear that, the first thing that comes to mind is being in the back seat of an Uber. The drivers are usually of East African heritage and they will automatically speak to me in a language that I do not know. They resolve that I am not deep into that part of my background. One driver in particular, who I ended up having a really good conversation with, this gentleman driving me, he kind of, he didn't scold me, but sort of did—this is why African women born in Canada are not a good thing, he implied; they lose themselves. But I have two parts to me.

Another instance, back when I was in elementary school, I frequently was not accepted by anybody. The other children of colour, they said, "You are white, you know that, right? You have basically light skin colour." But the Caucasian children were like, "You have darker skin."

I feel like [elementary school bullying] is sort of a right of passage. But I am stronger for it and I don't know who I'd be without that experience.

As far as maintaining those relations, I find that I don't. I know there's resolution and strength in knowing who I am, and at the end of the day—I've been told that it is dangerous mindset, but—I believe that all I need is me.

I'm not the most culturally accepted First Nations person, or the blackest Black person, or the queerest of queer people, but I have my own culture. My own Shammy-culture.

Wenzdae: Being a 'halfbreed' I am constantly challenged by my communities to prove that (1) I am 'one of them,' and (2) I understand the struggle to its fullest. People definitely push to find loopholes in my halfbreed-ness, to other me even further. Because I'm half Indigenous and half Black, I experience the struggles of both minorities daily. With community being a huge part of my life, I've had to learn how to distinguish people from the community. I've had many groups of people my age physically attack me on a basis of my skin; I'm still learning how to separate those people from a bigger and more loving community.

Kaya: When people challenge my lived experience, my automatic response is to get defensive. I am always shocked when people attempt to de-validate my truth, and I can think of countless moments throughout my life where this has happened. I seek to understand where that person is coming from. Ultimately, I hope to have a conversation where we both come out with a deeper understanding of one another.

Sometimes these situations stem from places of hurt or trauma. If the relationship is worth maintaining, I will put in effort to understand and empathize. But I do not always have the energy to have these conversations. It definitely depends on who is challenging me. People are not always open to listening. So sometimes the relationship is lost.

Share a story that feels true to you in the fullest way, or even a story in which you challenge stereotypes about you and your identities.

Shammy: I am going to tell the story about my mother. I was there [when it happened]. This is something that I think about a lot. She is the First Nations side of me. I do not know my father, which is a whole other story.

There is a thing called the Indian Affairs that determines if you are 'Native' enough. And back when I was thirteen, I needed braces. It was a nightmare of a situation, trying to get benefits. Services called—I heard the whole conversation because the volume was up very loud—and as soon as my mother was redirected to the Indian Affairs line, she was instantly accused of being on welfare. They assumed I did not have a second parent, and they questioned her about addictions, implying she would do something else with the money. This lady eventually looked my mother up and realized that my mother has been working hard her entire life. And the woman never apologized to my mother. Her tone flipped. My mother dealt with discrimination her entire life. Afterwards, she told me that that's how things are and it might be better some day, but having an Indigenous background is more of a curse than a blessing. My thirteen-year-old self wanted to pay for everything on my own from that day on. It's so interesting that that was my thought process and I saw how hard it was for my mom to deal with that.

Not every Indigenous person takes advantage of the system. We're not those people. So for me, at the time, that was eye-opening.

All the way back to elementary school, being Indigenous around that age is something that follows you all throughout the school system. Once you were in kindergarten, there's a box that goes on your file and you mark down whether you are First Nations, Metis, Inuit, or Not Applicable. I'm not sure if this is just something that's part of the Catholic Edmonton school board, but every year I had to fill it out and it continues until high school. And as I checked off First Nations, I thought, "I'm a good student. I'm not a liar. They just want to know."

Every single day I was pulled from class and asked if I needed help or extra tutoring and I said no. I was a pretty bright kid, but it changed after I marked that box. They assumed that my home wasn't a place where I could study; they even asked me that, outright. "I don't understand why you are not accepting this extra help," they would say, and that was an eye-opening moment for me too. I was about eight when I realized this is how [our] people are treated.

I tested out my theory and I wasn't going to check that box in school after grade five. And then it stopped. It stopped immediately. That to me was ridiculous and crazy, and I could see why that was ridiculous and crazy even at that age.

Simone: While writing this, I am totally burnt out from the last three days of life. And so I think the story I will tell is the story of my hectic schedule. Yesterday, I modelled for my friend's African clothing line at a fashion show. The clothing was made of beautiful, vibrant prints that were so bold you couldn't look away. Then, in the evening, I went to a community event to do Métis social dances. I usually wear moccasins and a long skirt when I dance at these events, but I wore one of the gorgeous printed shirts from my friend's line this time. This morning, I went to a photo shoot for burlesque photos and I was in six-inch heels and lingerie.

There was a time when I felt I couldn't be all of my selves at the same time. I ended up compartmentalizing my cultures a lot. Now, I know that I can dance traditional styles as well as more sensual styles like burlesque.

I can be Black in Indigenous spaces and Métis in African spaces. I can let all of my selves into the same room.

Wenzdae: Favouring my Bajan/Arawak features with virtually straight hair throws people off, a lot. For a long time I was seen as a 'faker' by those in the Toronto-based Indigenous community. With an absent father and immigrant grandparents, I didn't have many ties to the inner-city Black community. I always felt a bit in-between, and never fully included. When I would dance at powwows in my full regalia, people no longer saw me as Black—but that's not what I wanted a few years back. I was walking around the powwow grounds fully dressed with otter hair ties hanging from my braids. Two Black girls ran over to talk to me—which was common at powwows as many people had questions. She grabbed my hair tie, looked at me, back at the hair tie, and said, "Is this weave?" Surprisingly enough, years later, I haven't forgotten that, because it was the only time I felt like I didn't have to choose. I felt like she recognized who I was without me having to justify why I look the way I do.

Kaya: A story that feels especially true to me is the story of me comforting my dog as a toddler. When there was a thunderstorm, she went to go hide in the closet because she was so scared. I went and sat beside her, petting her and hugging her, making sure she was okay. I was about two, I think. My mom tells this story and notes it as being the first true sign of my intuitive empathic powers. This story makes me think of how, my whole life, I have been able to feel the emotions of other peoples as if they were my own. This is such an innate part of my being; it is my superpower. Though this is a gift, it also brings me a lot of pain. However, I cannot imagine living without this part of myself. It is what makes me such an effective artist, I think.

What does kinship mean to you?

Shammy: To me, when I think of the word kinship I immediately think of *Game of Thrones* [laughs], but I suppose, in my life, kinship means people who come together in one collective or a shared experience, cultural experience, personal experience, who share an adversity that you have.

I think kinship is the people you keep around you, who understand what your life means to you and they feel the same way.

Simone: I always say that community is the remedy for loneliness. Because we live in a capitalistic society that individualizes everybody and disconnect us from one another, it's so important to have ties. To me, kinship isn't necessarily about blood. It's about relationships that you nurture; it's about love. Kinship networks are some of the ways that we can hold each other up.

Through colonization, our intricate kinship ties have been scattered across continents and oceans. And a lot of people have small families or none at all. So the ability to re-create these kinship networks after being colonized is revolutionary. I have had many people in my life become like aunties, sisters, mothers, and grandparents to me, out of necessity and out of love.

Wenzdae: Kinship to me is the way we relate to one another; to choose to be family and not limit ourselves by nation or blood.

Kaya: Kinship to me is little strands of energy between people that glow and flow. Kinship is relationality. You can feel kinship; it is beyond blood. I felt a kinship to the ocean, even before I ever saw or submerged myself in it. The sun on my face through evergreens makes me feel a kinship to my ancestors. Kinship to me is connection, understanding, trust, compassion, and love. It fosters strength, solidarity, and resilience.

How do creativity and culture intersect for you in your life, if at all?

Shammy: Luckily, I am an artist, I am a dancer and an actor. For me, creativity and culture are always working together.

The writing I do—even if I don't share it with anyone—shows that too. I'm constantly in conflict because I don't want to be the person who creates art that represents my collective identities, but it often happens that way.

A good example of culture and creativity intersecting would be an art show that I was a part of this weekend [February 2018].

It was called the Chinook Series, in Edmonton, and I was in a piece that was made up entirely of Black artists from different places, titled "What Black Life Requires." It was a beautiful piece, fusing the experiences of [people of] African descent in Canada. Mostly poetry, but also dance through a narrative. It was a big ol' fun time and the most important piece that I've been involved in.

Culture, creativity, and art go hand in hand for me.

Simone: I believe that in many cultures, art doesn't simply exist for the purpose of art. There is usually a story to be told. I do a style of dance that's called Métis jigging. I've been taught that it's a cultural dance because the steps come from European styles with a Celtic influence, but it became popular in First Nation communities where they incorporated Indigenous steps from Turtle Island. So every time I dance, it's Métis culture brought alive. Every step has a certain place that it came from and a story to go with it, if you can find the right person to tell you.

So I believe that art is a part of culture and they're never really separate. For example, the beadwork that I wear wasn't meant to sit in a museum. It was meant to be worn day-to-day and become a part of life.

Wenzdae: My life revolves around culture and art. At fourteen, I started my own home-grown traditional Indigenous beadwork business, which fuelled my passion for design, business, and knowledge. Now, at eighteen, I've decided to use my knowledge passed down by my grandmothers to open my own African/Indigenous beauty business, mixing traditions with modern fashion and making a feeling of 'belonging' accessible to people like me.

Kaya: I feel as though I live and breathe creativity, and that my creativity is fed by all the cultures that I draw from. All the cultures that I participate in. Cultures that enrich my being. I am mixed Indigenous, Afro-Caribbean, and settler. I feel that I have many stories and secrets to uncover and explore that my ancestors have gifted to me. I feel myself unpacking, through art, all these facets that make up my identity. I understand the world through creativity, as I interpret things through writing, drawing, making music, painting—making in general. I reflect upon my creations constantly in terms of what they can reveal about my understanding of my cultures and ultimately myself. I constantly think about the history of creation in my cultures as well. Creation stories, foods, garments, baskets, hairstyles, music. I think about how these integral forms of creating were such a natural part of life, how these forms of creating are rooted in philosophies of relationality and reciprocity. How does the way in which I create honour and practice these ways of making? How can I carry on the legacies of my ancestors through my art? These are considerations I take very seriously when creating.

What are some things in this universe that bring you joy?

Shammy: Sweatpants that fit properly. My sister, she brings me a lot of joy. Home brings me joy. Whatever that means to me at the time, it changes always. Being understood, that brings me a lot of joy. Cheese pizza. Those are all the important ones, I think.

Simone: Because I live such a busy and chaotic life, I'm all over the place doing something different every day. So when I can follow a routine, that brings me joy. When I've soaked in the bath, cooked dinner, cleaned my room, washed the dishes and e-transferred the rent to my landlord, I feel happy and satisfied. When I can talk with my sister on the phone for three hours, that brings me joy. Oh, and sipping from a big mug of chai tea in sweatpants after a long day. That is perfection.

Wenzdae: One thing that brings me joy in this universe is knowing that I am the product of my ancestors' wildest dreams.

Kaya: What brings me joy? The smell of rain, big clouds in an evening summer sky, my cats, citronella, fresh peaches, my family's support of my art endeavours, my boyfriend's laugh, hearing a really good song for the first time, elders in fabulous outfits, spoken word, making a fire... there are countless things that bring me joy. I could fill a book with lists of things that bring me joy. When I remember all these things, it is like I am lighting candles inside myself. All these candles bring light to me and help me to avoid all of the deep, dark spaces within myself. Although these are necessary spaces to navigate, even to dwell in for a little while, I am so grateful to have so many different candles that I can light. I feel grateful to have so much joy in my life. To be able to see, touch, feel, smell, taste, hear, and transmit all of the joy that exists in the universe. This is one of the greatest gifts I have been given.

BLACK WRITERS MATTER

SISTER **VISION**

BLACK WOMEN AND WOMEN OF COLOUR PRESS

Lecture from Writing in Dangerous Times: Survival,
Resistance, Joy, Conference (October 28, 2017, Toronto)

— MAKEDA SILVERA —

I t's great to be here and to share the company of you all. I thank the organizers for their hard work in pulling this conference together and for inviting me to this much anticipated community-based conference with such an important theme: "Writing in Dangerous Times: Survival, Resistance, Joy." It is an important, appropriate, and engaging theme, particularly in the times we live in. It reminds me of the lyrics of the late Jamaican singer Bob Marley: "Dem belly full, but we hungry." And that feeling is even physical. We're still hungry to be heard, hungry to be counted in, hungry to be heeded. Since Sister Vision shut down, our portion has been very small indeed. That portion is miniscule for first-time writers, particular those of working-class backgrounds and from the LGBTQ of colour communities.

I have been asked to speak about Sister Vision: Black Women and Women of Colour Press—its beginnings in 1985, its contributions to Canadian literature and culture, its sixteen years in the trenches.

When Sister Vision was founded in 1985, it was in part because of the near invisibility of women of colour in the Canadian literary landscape—it was as if we were a blur. Our stories weren't being printed, our voices remained unheard, never mind being acknowledged or celebrated. But although this was challenging, it was not so forceful as to make the dream of the press impossible. Still, we were always reminded of the limits that circumscribed our work, not the least of which were the biases within the industry and lingering racism.

Although alternative presses and white women's presses had sprung up in the early 1980s, those presses were not particularly interested in publishing us: our voices didn't sound like theirs. And, for the most part, questions of class and colour were not important parts of white women's feminist analysis.

In 1984 we could count on one hand the number of Black women in Canada who had single-authored books or were featured in anthologies. Disgraceful, when we look back at Black people's early arrival in Canada and at our contributions in all manner of work, including publishing. I am speaking here specifically of Mary Ann Shadd, an American-born anti-slavery activist, who came to Canada in 1852, where she edited *The Provincial Freeman*. She later became a teacher, then a lawyer, and a campaigner for women's suffrage. Shadd was the first Black woman publisher in all of North America.

When Sister Vision Press was founded, there was a growing community of Black women and women of colour who were feminist and also LGBTQ, women who wanted to write, to illustrate books, and to learn the ropes of publishing in a safe and encouraging environment.

The first book Sister Vision published in 1985 was *Speshal Rikwes,* a book of poetry by Ahdri Zhina Mandiela. Its significance was that its language was 'experimental,' in that it was written in the Jamaican language, Patois, which is often mistakenly called a 'dialect.' We began as we meant to go on: the phrase "Speshal Rikwes" is a call for appreciation and respect. Not only would this first book by Sister Vision Press be groundbreaking, it signalled that we were about taking risks.

Between 1985 and 2001, Sister Vision—a small press by and for women of colour—had published over 75 first-time writers in book-length works and over 200 women in anthologies. Many of these, too, were first-time writers. Not an easy feat. With only three staff at any one time, we worked twelve-hour days at times, particularly during production. We also had to contend with an unstable fiscal base, juggling many debts. We did a lot of fundraising. In those days there was no such thing as social media. We walked and walked and walked, posting flyers on street poles, used word of mouth and telephone trees, mailed out flyers, attended events and handed out flyers there too. We could rely on a steady stream of volunteers who were eager to give of their time. It was also an exciting time, very in-the-moment, building a community with people and words. Sister Vision opened up spaces and offered writing workshops.

One of my fondest memories is getting the first box of books from the printer, cracking it open, and smelling that newness. Over those years we forged alliances with Black women, Indigenous women, Caribbean and Asian women, both in Canada and internationally, and our books bear testimony to that. Sister Vision published a wide range of books—novels, short stories, essays, anthologies, plays, academic works, and children's books.

I particularly remember Lenore Keeshig-Tobias's children's book, *Bineshiinh Diabajimovin: Bird Talk*. As managing editor I immediately said yes to its gentle strength. *Bineshiinh Diabajimovin: Bird Talk* was published in Ojibway—or, to be current, in Anishinaabe—and English. The book deals with an incident where school children are playing cowboys and Indians. When the young Indigenous character says that it's not a good game to play, her friends immediately question in a curious fashion her identity as an Indigenous person. The book's clean, simple, black-and-white illustrations were done by the author's daughter, Polly Keeshig-Tobias. *Bineshiinh Diabajimovin: Bird Talk* won the Martin Luther King's I Have a Dream Award at a school in Manhattan.

Another of my favourite children's books is *Crabs for Dinner* by Ghanaian-Canadian writer Adwoa Badoe. A young girl, first-generation Canadian, hates the very idea of eating crab, wonders how her grandmother and mother can possibly love it, but eventually tastes it, after her family describes its wonderful flavour. Althea Prince's *How the Starfish Got to the Sea* is another delightful tale.

For me the books that best represent Sister Vision Press were our anthologies because they gave voice to many women, and these were women from a wide range of backgrounds. The anthologies let Sister Vision introduce many first-time writers, writers I knew very few publishers would take the time to encourage, to nurture. For example, *Piece of My Heart*, published in 1991, was a first: a groundbreaking anthology charting the experiences of women of colour through poetry and prose testimonies. The voices of Caribbean women living in Canada rang out loud and strong. *Creation Fire* brought together the poetry of both English-speaking and non-English-speaking Caribbean women in Canada and internationally. *Lionheart Gal* revealed the life stories of Jamaican women and, like *Speshal Rikwes*, was written entirely in the Jamaican language, Patois. The women of *Lionheart Gal* were at the time all part of the Sistren Theatre Collective and all came from working-class roots.

Black Girl Talk, a collection of writings by young Black women, was also the first of its kind and spoke with raw, sincere honesty of the challenges young Black women of all sexual orientations and backgrounds faced. Another very significant anthology was *The Colour of Resistance: A Contemporary Collection of Writing by Aboriginal Women*, published in 1993. In the book's foreword, editor Connie Fife declares, "Within the pages of this anthology are words that carry their own life, having been birthed through the voices of Aboriginal women who have chosen to re-invent how we resist, how we refuse to be silenced." The anthology's contributors were drawn from Canada and the United States and defy the limitations of borders.

Miscegenation Blues, published in 1994, brought together the voices of mixed-race women and was another first in North America. In naming the anthology, the editor, Carol Camper, asserts both her activism and her rejection of the white mainstream connotations of the word 'miscegenation.' The anthology *Some Black Women: Profiles of Black Women in Canada* was not cutting edge by some feminist standards, but was important because it documented Black women's individual achievements as well as their collective ones, and provided hitherto lacking histories of early Black women's clubs, Black churches, and Black landmarks. The books featured profiles of dedicated Black women who have contributed to Canada. Many of the women were unknown and unsung heroes; others were well-known figures in the mainstream straight Black community.

But Where Are You From? Stories of Identity and Assimilation in Canada brought together thirty women from across Canada to discuss, debate, challenge, and respond to this unfortunately very common question. The editor, Hazelle Palmer, the daughter of Caribbean immigrants, was born in London, England, and immigrated to Canada as a child. This was a question she herself was asked many times, although she has no discernable Caribbean or English accent. The book moves the discussion of identity and belonging forward.

Afrika Solo, by Djanet Sears, was the first play Sister Vision published. Traditionally, publishers are extremely cautious about publishing poetry and plays because they do not sell well. But because we as publishers had also signed up to take risks, we welcomed the script.

This one-woman play chronicles a young Black woman's voyage of self-discovery. The protagonist heads off for Afrika after her best friend tells her, "Go back to where you come from." In the playwright's words, "I was born in Britain but did not belong. Where in fact did I belong? I am a naturalized citizen of Canada. What do I answer when people constantly ask me where I'm from? The Caribbean? Even though I have never lived there? Which of my parents' countries should I choose?"

Sister Vision began in dangerous times. We gained some ground but we still have a way to go to fill that hunger. I look forward to other Black women and women of colour picking up the baton and carrying us forward in publishing.

When I look back on the years at Sister Vision, at the time I lived and breathed publishing, I am astounded by the volume of books we put out. But even more so, nearly twenty years have passed since we shut our doors and our books are still relevant. Imagine if we were still publishing? We were way ahead of our time.

BECOMING **POETRY**
QUEER BLACKNESS AS THE
FULL ABSORPTION OF LIGHT

— *Sapphire Woods* —

By the end of my senior undergraduate year, I had come into my queerness first and my Blackness second. I was infatuated with Jeanette Winterson because she was the first queer female author I had read that felt familiar to my growing consciousness. Her book, *The Stone Gods*, talked about space and futurism and that, somewhere in between nothing and everything, was the promise of dark matter; blackness—the full absorption of light. In the perceived light years it had taken me to come to this awakening, I thought I had caught a glimpse of myself. I was connecting Deleuze and Guattari's theories of rhizomatic ways of being—nonlinear, sporadic, manifesting (1987). Together with Winterson, I was forming a deeper, clearer image of myself before my very eyes.

And it was good.

Until I read Adrienne Rich. And then I read an interview Rich had with Audre Lorde. Then I read Audre Lorde, and bell hooks, and started reading *A Bridge Called My Back* by Cherrìe Morraga and Gloria E. Anzaldúa, and read and read. I was no longer shadowed by the dark side of the moon but basked fully in its illumination where histories and stories did not just allude to but belonged to my reality as a Black lesbian. I was falling upwards into a skyless world where white women were teaching me that love, although in secret, could bloom. At one time, the Winterson texts modelled women who met under guises and darkness. These women's lives were as much a secret to themselves as they were to the gazes of surveillance and fear of punishment they passed under. Simultaneously, bell hooks became a grounding source in reconnecting me to a source of self-loving light that I could not find in isolation.

I first came out to myself in Edmonton. Alberta summer days can be beautiful, but the light merely fringed the perimeter of a creeping darkness that began to burgeon as depression. On numerous dusks I would visit The End of the World—a storey-high elevated sidewalk along the Saskatchewan River that dropped off suddenly into space.

Before the sun began its descent, I would stand close to the edge and look up at the endless Alberta clouds and imagine what freedom would look like. Did freedom look like a slow revolution, noted in the way the clouds blew with the sky's convection currents? Did it look like the End of the World—a solitary sudden drop into the space below and into fast moving water? Or did freedom look like the precipice before the End?

Was freedom both space, but past the clouds, and among clusters of stars? Night without sleep became the plane where I imagined possibilities open to me. If I chose to take after the white women in the stories I read, and absorbed the darkness of depression, I would never know what was past the weight of nothingness. I remember reading *A Bridge Called My Back* and sewed Gloria Anzaldua's question like a life jacket to the inside of my chest: "*¿Qué hacer de aquí y cómo? What to do from here and how?*" Anzaldúa asks whether or not women of colour are tired of suffering and if we want to come out of the shadows of our silences and pain. I remember the piercing light that blazed from that question. No answer, no promise, but a possibility of light that made me choose to not leave myself in order to find life, but instead, go into the depths of myself to see what could be created.

The life I was building with my first same-sex partner was indeed a star, one that burst into an entire, whole world. Although this planet was full of life, we still combated isolation like the gravity of a black hole. Before C (my first partner, of West-Indian descent) and I moved in together, we lived in a dormitory at our conservative, Christian university. I remember a time when both of us were working, trying to save money to move off campus. It was after another ten-hour day, while I was showering, when C answered a bang on the door. It was the dorm deans, who thought that they smelled weed and assumed it would definitely be us. I was called out of the shower, where I was washing my hair, so they could search our room. We stood frozen, under surveillance, under scrutiny. We stood, my hands up, protecting the appearance of my hair rather than my body—all of my dignity up for examination. When they left, they left with nothing. My heart was in my throat and there was a sense of urgency to move.

After that summer, we did move. By chance, C and I found an apartment loft above a house off campus. Within this space we made a home. The hyper-visibility of both my queerness and Blackness contesting with the fight against my erasure. This began the catalyst in my search for Black and of-colour women writers. I was ravenous to find someone who understood the transformation, the alchemy, of what it is to come into one's queer Blackness. I had already chosen to live once, so I rose to the responsibility of living, namely as a Black, queer woman. In the midst of isolation, I replayed bell hooks in my mind like a mantra: "In the face of barriers we still have the capacity to invent our lives, to shape our destinies in ways that maximize our well-being" (2000, 57).

Under this charge, I started to reframe the orbit of my senior undergrad paper. The stories of women loving women written by white writers did not reflect the life that I was forming for myself out of nothing. I was reading hooks and Lorde, who had literally saved my life—who had already lived lives of transformation in the midst of erasure and the violence of imposed isolation. They taught me that, in my depression, I could mine light from the changes that were happening within me. Lorde anticipated that, under the simultaneous scrutiny and erasure of my existence, I could "learn to use the products of that scrutiny for power within our living, [and] those fears which rule our lives and form our silences begin to lose their control over us" (36). My fear was becoming the sad, white women in the Winterson stories. I wanted to become something of the light that was keeping me alive. I was using my literary ancestors and guides to explore both my queerness and Blackness and to resist imposed deaths.

While I read and organized these thoughts, I was also met with the injustice of the hidden canon of my history; classics that informed the origins of my thoughts on how I could come to be loved, seen, resist, and survive. Before the end of the winter semester, I approached my supervisor in all the splendour of my ancestry and proposed that I used Lorde, Morraga, and hooks as the foundation of my arguments. I wanted to write using only women of colour that supported my thoughts, who knew me before I was even born.

My supervisor told me I was too late.

My senior paper was due too soon to change my framework, my foundation. Sitting in the supervisor's office with those books in my hands, I was furious. My heart was breaking. I had been betrayed. I was afforded the academic exploration of queerness as something edgy and useful to make my department relevant. But under the refracted Whiteness of the queer rainbow, my Blackness was omitted. A semester later, under the weight of invisibility, I presented my senior undergrad paper half-heartedly, with pats on the back for using postcolonial theory.

With the degree I proclaimed myself a self-taught colonizer of my own mind.

My identity, separated, was conquered at the hands of white minds and experiences sitting nostalgic in the face of suffering. I was complicit in the destruction and dissemination of the resource-rich territories that I was just beginning to cultivate. I, colonizer, did not know that these Black lesbian writers existed before I discovered them, and so I felt that I had lost out on the gift of humanity that I could receive.

Again, I could feel myself fragmenting. I had done the work of reconciling queerness and Blackness in myself. I had withstood extreme isolation and become my own light. I was trying to show that both queerness and Blackness were the fundamental elements of life made after death. For a moment, I thought that my reality—post Lorde, hooks, and Moraga—would be emancipatory. After two years of silencing and imposed isolation, I would look at this paper that spoke my truth with confidence. This paper would recognize the history of queer, Black female erasure. But there was no postcolonialism. These histories I still carried in my body, in my relationships, in the ways that I love, and in the ways that I create life for myself. The texts and words that had kept me alive would only do just that in this moment.

Although there is no postcolonialism, it was Donna Kate Rushin who commanded: "Stretch or drown/Evolve or die" (1981, xxii). There was still the responsibility of reconstructing the forced fragmentations into constellations—decolonizing my mind and reconciling what parts had been used with the pieces discarded sans request. I chose to live the truth of possibility—the possibility of reconciliation, the possibility of myself with myself. "We awakened our gods and we left them there, because we never needed gods again" (Sharpe 2016, 17). In the face of dead, white gods and erasure, I found god—not outside of myself, not at the precipice of another new beginning, but in myself. And I loved her, fiercely.

In the end, we did resist erasure. Without announcement or fanfare, C and I moved, in mourning of not ever being held safely or guided with healing hands. When we moved, we moved the perspective of what was possible for ourselves and all who took a taste of our magick. There was no coming out, no acknowledgement of the work we were doing, just the deafening silence of our wake.

I remember, on a cool autumn evening C and I went for a walk and I brought the rose quartz I had been keeping under my pillow from the past summer. I frantically needed to call in love for myself. The rainbow of refracted white queerness was not enuf. Being in rural Alberta, there were no queers of colour to guide me through the passage I was moving through. I had considered suicide but could not dash the possibility of futurity. The rose quartz had all my love and loss wrapped up inside of it. Somehow, in the waters of rage and pain, I had surfaced, if momentarily, to find love that pushed me forward and celebrated the life I had grown into. On our walk together, C and I buried the rose quartz beneath the newly planted trees that lined the path towards the campus's church. We laughed, considering the possibility of our love, manifesting, rising from the earth and terrorizing all those who crossed this path.

In a way, our love did manifest and made waves for ourselves and the entire microcosm we lived in with our intention-filled movement. These waves, or wakes, as Christina Sharpe defines them, "allow those among the living to mourn the passing of the dead through ritual....But wakes are also...the disturbance caused by a body swimming, or one that is moved, in water; the air currents behind a body in flight" (2016, pp). Instead of taking cues from the white, queer women in Winterson's books, who were left broken, mourning, and lost, I decided to wake and rise.

Together, C and I, we inspired shifts in perspective and, apart, we thrived in our areas of study and expanded our goals and dreams. If, at any time, you as a Black, queer woman are the only one who knows the legitimacy and alchemy of your worth, let it be so. I am Black, I define my life as a woman, I recreate and nurture love between women, and I create and birth possibility and new worlds within what is dead and dying. The poetry of my Black existence is in resistance to colonial, white nihilism and defeatism canonized as education. The poetry of my Black, queer existence is resistant; it stands and moves as a living monument of Black, queer waking and dream-making. Where a wake encompasses mourning, a wake is also movement, it is energy enough to generate the quality of light I need in order to pursue my own magick.

In adjusting the quality of light by which to view my own queer Blackness for myself, I became light. In the passing of old lives came the movement of new possibility—I was, and am, becoming poetry.

REFERENCES

Deleuze, G., and F. Guattari. 1987. *A Thousand Plateaus*. Minneapolis: University of Minnesota Press.

hooks, b. 2000. *All About Love*. New York: HarperCollins.

Moraga, C., and G.E. Anzaldúa, eds. 1981. *The Bridge Called My Back*. London: Persephone Press.

Rushin, D. 1981. "The Bridge Poem." In *The Bridge Called My Back*, edited by C. Moraga and G.E. Anzaldúa. London: Persephone Press.

Shange, N. 1975. *For Colored Girls Who Have Considered Suicide/When the Rainbow is Enuf.* New York: Simon & Schuster.

Sharpe, C. 2016. *In the Wake: On Blackness and Being.* Durham, NC: Duke University Press.

Winterson, J. 2007. *The Stone Gods.* London: Hamish Hamilton.

MEMORIALTY

— Christelle Saint-Julien —

Originally published on the blog Le Shindig

A friend lent a book to me, insisting vividly that I read it. *Ongoingness, The End of a Diary,* by Sarah Manguso is a personal essay on the course of a diary that was kept through her life. You could call it a memoir as well. "I couldn't face the end of a day without a record of everything that had ever happened,"(2015, 3) the author recounts.

This friend had spotted a tendency of mine that I never had before: a propensity to document every aspect of my life that I, randomly, judge worthy of retaining. I would not know exactly what and why; it is an analysis that would require the documenting of my documentation process. My approach is not a neat one, it goes from visual notes to writing, book notes to screens—as long as it is somewhere. Odd thing is, I rarely revisit my personal archive, as if the gesture itself was more of a mechanism of habit, a compulsion. This penchant I have for recollection makes me estranged from the concept of ephemerality. I could never understand the appeal of Snapchat, Instagram stories, a Buddha board, or even performance art.

"I wanted to end each day with a record of everything that had ever happened," Manguso recounts. Just like her, I am terrified of what I cannot remember, similarly to how I continuously misplace the daily objects of my life and genuinely forget to call someone back or bring something I was supposed to get. But I would remember what someone said that day, or how it made me feel a decade ago, or where I was when it happened. This selective memory is my shield, as well as my pride—I can defend and justify myself really well through confusion or I can easily put things into perspective. But the weight of such a memory makes it difficult for me to compartmentalize. Too much information weighs on effectiveness.

The memory of the oldest person I am close to, a life full of lives and experiences I cannot even fathom, is a story observed in real time. My dad, who was born in the forties, never speaks about the past, except when asked to. It is as if nothing that took place was memorable, in the naive sense of the word, as if joy and good times were always around the corner despite the greatest difficulties. As clueless as he can be about the course of things, he never seemed fazed by anything he did not know.

I believe that my father's brain was wired to strictly remember the important stuff. In his case that means places (he drove a taxi for over thirty years and never used a GPS) and people (his family and friends he made over a long life spent in several countries), which seems enough in a context of survival. Modernity never touched him. ATM machines were never his friends, he never learned how to use a computer, he does not know what Apple products are (despite the fact that I even worked for that company for years), he doesn't know what Facebook implies— and that is just fine. I myself encouraged this behaviour, admiring how simple it makes life. As intense as everything always is for me, all seems surrounded by calm and kindness around him.

We always yearn for what we cannot have.

Witnessing fragments of memory leaving someone is a hard scene. A mind that does not remember causes panic. My dad started losing his memory due to old age and illness, and he sensed that he was starting to forget that he was forgetting.

Deliberately remembering allows you to rewrite the narrative. It is my own story that I'm trying to recount, to understand situations through and in the time, place, and people that made and shape me. Something happening now is different from the same thing happening another time. In retrospect, I'm looking for something that is mine alone and that can exist in the bigger picture.

You can alter the facts—make them easier to bear or more spiteful, toss the negative, loop the memorable, make room for epiphanies. You find the capacity to articulate feelings based on past experience.

You can tie stories together, you can discard others, project a situation, realize how you never learn or how history repeats itself—and damn yourself if you won't do anything about it. Dream of realities, from the reality of these dreams.

Then, what do you choose to remember, and why? In my case, not that I like to admit it, it's a gesture of control—I am, consciously or not, carefully selecting the memories. By documenting I am not making anything; rather, I am transforming, analyzing, learning, re-contextualizing, validating. I don't document in fear of FOMO (a millennial term for fear of missing out), it is more in the nature of questioning, looking for a consensus: am I the only one who sees things the way I see them?

In my internal process lies a dismal dysfunction of mine. Writing is a compulsion that I perfected into a purpose and a salary. I write because I don't know how to be. When I write, I can be anything, including who I am. I try to remember what is done and how it is done because I am trying to mimic the world in which I'm living. I lack this understanding of social codes and customary behaviour of the world that surrounds me. Social interactions don't come to me naturally. I dramatically lack tact. I am terrible at having normal conversations. The capacity to remember and to draw from these memories renders itself a backdrop for small talk. I can dodge questions and communicate empathy in a way that feels more sincere and reliable than just my reaction.

Recollection of memories is also a matter of going through things deeply rather than staying on the surface. What is the meaning of these things I am seeing, and why do I feel an urge to pin them down? It's less about sharing than it is about keeping. Sharing, in my case, happens in words—a story told, a caption, a status, an essay.

In this vein, part of my person, including my profession as a writer, is anchored in the stationary. Reflecting on this fact, memories and experiences do not make me a forward-looking person by definition, as I am only in opposition, switching paths or gears after trials and tribulations. I don't do well with disruption, and upon change, I often need preparation or a moment, long or short, of dwelling. I am a walking reminiscence, anchored in our present time.

There is a conversation about our capacity of retaining, in this age of abundance of news and stimuli. What happens inside of us when the mind remembers?

Memory is desperately intangible, despite the amount of time, conscious or not, we spend remembering—from where your keys are to the ways of someone you lost. Remembering, in itself, is not an emotion, neither is it a reaction, although one almost invariably causes one or the other. Yet, memory is one of the elements that strikes us and shapes us the most as human beings.

I cannot tell if my dad's constant worry—what did you eat today—directly translates to, "I remember what hunger feels and I do not want you to ever have to live through it, if it be only for a second," or if it's less dramatic than I imagine, if he is simply curious to know. Nor do I ask him if he retains that information, for he asks me the question as often as he asks, "How was your day?" when we speak on the phone, which is several times a week.

Memory is a curse for the resilient, the exile's sole baggage on a long migration road. In a life of displacement, it can pain you to remember. But how do we find our way home if we can't remember? In my parents' oral culture, hailing from Haïti, nothing is written down. You just know what you know and what you were told. Upon migration, you are left with the history of where you come from as proof of your existence. A new identity is forcibly built for and around you through the eyes of your new surroundings. But you cannot forget what becomes known as 'before,' or 'back home,' or 'when I was'. These identity claims are rare, out of survival. They have chosen not to speak out in order to protect their children and themselves: a survival tactic adopted under the insidious promulgation that things are better here and this way. And myself, with a foot in each culture, born in Montreal, a city where the Haitian diaspora lives strong, I'm trying the grasp all of the untold stories for archiving purposes. What is this unexplainable heritage I am relentlessly trying to unpack? If my place of existence is secured and settled, my mind still wanders, trying to trace back the path others walked silently to lead me here, safe. I know which oceans they crossed and the land they walked, but I wish to know where their minds have been.

Still, more questions remain. What has been forgotten? What is remembered? Even as my dad cannot remember my address or my birthday, he insists that he is not forgetting me, although it's harder now to reach out since he cannot remember how to use his smartphone. He remembers how to hide the truth from me, about his health, his state, his autonomy. He remembers how anxious I can be.

Writing is an old-school medium. It is ancient, reliable, resistant to change. Truth is, I find it hard to be in touch with my time. I wish I could plunge into my father's memory, turning it into art, into a book, into an essay, into tweets or an Instagram feed. I wish I could use it as my comfort when I'm tired of my own narrative. But memory does not save anything in time. We don't stay the same.

Paradoxically, the more you know, the less you are prone to forget. That is why we learn to remember better.

There are certainly benefits in forgetting. I call it lightness; it can be compared to the bliss of ignorance. You can flush the bad, and that is, ultimately, a luxury. What we remember does not matter, in a sense. I am forcing myself to forget. Forget how worried I am, forget how I make a big deal of everything, forget how much I fail. When it comes to my dad, I only want to remember the positive, childishly pushing away reality.

I cannot wrap my head around this eulogy I am constantly making, neither am I capable of conceiving a future. I want to remember the why and the how in the mundane, a mundane so full of colours, of laughter, of words and nuance and emotions that the world around me seems to be at worst blind, at best inattentive to what the 'other' is living.

I am trying to put one plus one together, how it came into life and what was before so that I am here today and I keep existing, as a witness and as a result of joys and sacrifices. And I see you. I see you before the memory dies. I am accountable to you, who are denied a happy ending, a dream. I'm trying to express, in my way, that your story won't die with you. That it touched me.

As long as I can write, I have a constant access to my memory, to my dreams and thoughts, to how my days were spent. I write to forget. I write to carry on. I write to make sense of things. In the greater sense of things, I would, strangely, want to be forgotten. I'm amazed and puzzled when people remember me or my work. Memories keep a trail of one's life and this is the life of an absurd person who has memories as quickly as they die.

The joy in the voice of my dad when he hears my voice for the first time on any given day is a happiness that can't be faked. It has remained unchanged for as long as I can remember, and it is a gift that I carry along with me every day. Is it a memory if constantly actualized, yet unchanged? My father always has this joke, when we haven't talked for a couple of days, he dramatically exclaims, "It's been years!" A declaration that, coming from him, is more absurd in its tone than the statement. Just like memories, time is also a question of perception.

FICTION IS NOT FRIVOLOUS

A LECTURE

— H. NIGEL THOMAS —

Delivered at the Morrin Centre in Quebec City on April 6, 2013.

n this lecture I use the words poetry and fiction loosely. When we hear the word fiction, we think of prose. However, the original meaning of poet was: one who invents using language.

I begin with three quotations. (1) "[Poets] measure the circumference and sound the depths of human nature with a comprehensive and all-penetrating spirit...[They] are the unacknowledged legislators of mankind" (Shelley 1967, 1085). (2) "Aristotle, I have been told, has said that poetry is the most philosophic of all writing: it is so: its object is truth...which gives confidence to the tribunal to which it appeals....The obstacles which stand in the way of the fidelity of the biographer and historian...are incalculably greater than those which are to be encountered by the poet who comprehends the dignity of his art" (Wordsworth 1967, 325). (3) "Since the truth of human experience is concentrated and preserved best through literary art, it is mainly the black author and his public interpreter, the critic, who will inspire their race toward its destiny" (Emmanuel 1971, 185). Shelley and Wordsworth, who were contemporaries, made these statements in answer to critics who felt that works of the imagination were second class.

James Emmanuel's statement was made in a different context: at the beginning of the 1970s, when it was understood that all of Black America should contribute to the liberation struggle ongoing in the United States and in Africa. There emerged at the time what was dubbed the Black Arts Movement. Its manifesto was to show Blacks everywhere a way of life different from the one Occidentals had imposed on them.

These writers stressed community over individualism, respect for nature, and a deeper understanding of the psychological benefits of African or African-derived rituals, and they did so for the most part through poetry and theatre. Houston Baker informs us that, at its height,

> mass black audiences turned out for readings by black authors in Harlem, Philadelphia, Washington, DC and elsewhere. And the most convincing evidence [of its relevance] was provided by the kinds of literary works that black people from all walks of life began to demand from publishers....It did indeed seem as though black literature had found its communal voice and that its writers had contributed to a radical modification of the acculturative process—a modification that allowed black meaning to move into the foreground. (Baker 1980, 128–129)

The works of writers like Toni Morrison, Alice Walker, Gloria Naylor, Leon Forrest—too many to enumerate—show the strong influences of the Black Arts Movement.

Liberation from oppression, external and internal, has always been at the core of African and African diasporic literature.

There's a special kind of knowledge that comes from fiction. Let us take, for example, Richard Wright's *Black Boy*, published in 1945. Even after reading numerous tomes of history and sociology about Blacks living under Jim Crow, one would still need *Black Boy* to understand

Jim Crow's impact on the psyches of those who lived under it. For the same reason, I would recommend Chinua Achebe's novels to anyone wishing to learn about the impact of British colonialism on the Ibo of Nigeria. There is an ongoing debate about whether Abraham Lincoln wrote that Harriet Beecher Stowe's *Uncle Tom's Cabin* was "the author of this great war," i.e. the United States Civil War.* However, there's no debate about the profound impact of *Uncle Tom's Cabin* on the anti-slavery campaign in the United States. What the story about Lincoln acknowledges is the power of fiction to motivate others—in this case to end oppression. To understand the ethos of classical Greece, we read Homer, Euripides, Aeschylus, Aristophanes, et al. It is noteworthy that philosophers like Schopenhauer, Nietzsche, Sartre, and Camus resorted to fiction to humanize what would otherwise be abstract philosophical formulations.

I am therefore astonished by the large number of people, usually Black, who tell me implicitly and explicitly that writing fiction is a puerile activity. We writers of fiction do exactly what Emmanuel and Wordsworth say: we record human experience in a manner different from historians, sociologists, and anthropologists. Among the many things that fiction does, I note the following: it bears witness to our times, it reflects the inner and outer forces that sustain or threaten to destroy us, and it constantly reminds us of what we are.

I would like at this point to emphasize the value of African-Canadian authors to a Canadian audience, both Black and white. Those of us who are Black are aware that Euro-Canadians have us at the lowest stratum in their schema of human value. With this ascription of value comes a dominant narrative with powerful tropes: primitive, backward, intellectually inferior, etc. While this perception still regulates how the dominant culture interacts with us—for example, paying us less for our labour, declaring our art to be inferior, our intellectual work to be less stellar—nowadays such notions are rarely overtly

---

* https://wraabe.wordpress.com/2008/06/26/abraham-lincoln-to-harriet-beecher-stowe-the-author-of-this-great-war/

expressed, and only get into the public discussion when an ad or sports commentator or some publicity-seeking persona expresses what the dominant culture believes and acts upon but would rather not talk about. Such attitudes are encrypted in the narratives of daily interaction, so, for example, twenty or thirty years ago, Black employees in white workplaces would be subject to, for example, a barrage of racist black jokes. The jokes themselves comprise the narrative that reifies the perception. When Blacks who were subjected to these demeaning jokes made light of them, they were commended for having a good sense of humour, which in essence meant that they understood that whites had the power to humiliate them with impunity. Thankfully, this rarely happens now. Those who would still like to be able to do so freely complain about the restrictiveness of political correctness. Still omnipresent, however, are the daily reminders that Blackness is marginal to Euro-American and Euro-Canadian culture. In Canada, if you have black skin and kinky hair, you are deemed to be from a country or continent known as Where-Are-You-From? In French: *T'es d'où?* When I lived in Quebec City, Blacks there were barraged with this question daily. A friend of mine, who taught at Champlain Regional College, left a teaching position she loved and went to live in Toronto, because, she said, this question felt like an assault on her being. She was born in Saint-Adele, from a Caucasian mother and a Black father. No one who asked her that question was satisfied with that answer. There was always a follow-up question: But where are you *really* from? Which she translated to mean: you are Black, you cannot truly claim Canadian roots. You are marginal to this culture. She left Quebec City the year before the publication of Lawrence Hill's *Black Berry, Sweet Juice* (2001), which thoroughly analyzes the attitudes underlying this question. In my own case, I decided to have a bit of fun with where-are-you-from? I answered: 'The Earth. And you?' Eventually I stopped, after coming close to being beaten up. And sometimes it got troubling: my friend and I were both asked, on different occasions, how it was that we had such excellent jobs, weren't there qualified Canadians to fill those positions?

Let me elaborate further on the dominant narrative by recounting another personal experience. In February 1988, the Quebec Human Rights Commission invited me to give a talk on Black ontology. I seized the opportunity to challenge the notion that, until the arrival of Europeans, Africans were trapped in the Stone Age. Culling information from works by Leo Frobenius, Cheik Anta Diop, Basil Davidson, Ivan Sertima, et al., I argued that Blacks were certainly not backward. On the day of the lecture, a reporter from *La Presse* read my speech before I delivered it and accused me of creating a fiction to embellish the African past. Nothing I told her swayed her from that opinion. I'd anticipated this. I'd had a foretaste in Quebec City. I'd asked an acquaintance there to check the paper for possible mistakes in the French, and he told me that he was shocked by my false claims. He worked in the Quebec public service—still does—and asked if he could share the paper with his colleagues. I told him yes. The larger the audience, the better, I felt. From his report, they called my findings pathetic, deranged assertions. This friend questioned a few of his acquaintances who'd lived in Africa, and from what they told him, he now seems to have a more nuanced view. Back to the *La Presse* reporter. I don't remember her name. I begged her to wait, because I had a short video that features Basil Davidson discussing the Iron Age in Africa. She stayed, saw the video, and apologized to me afterwards. She did further research and wrote a piece about it in *La Presse*. I went to that lecture knowing that, as a Black man, my white audience would not take the facts I presented seriously, unless they had been authenticated by whites. This deeply ingrained bias made Harvard professor Derrick Bell wonder, in *Faces at the Bottom of the Well: The Permanence of Racism* (1992), whether references written by him on others' behalf had any value.

What I have stated in the foregoing are facts that Blacks know to varying degrees, but they are, in addition to many other preoccupations, facts that Black poets, playwrights, and fiction writers embody in their characters. For, to be a serious writer one must get behind the facade of what passes for reality; much of the time that face masks reality. It therefore pains me when Blacks—oftentimes holders of university degrees—say they don't read fiction, that fiction is frivolous. Others say that life is hard and books about Black reality are depressing and therefore to be avoided. The latter statement usually leaves me speechless. All the Black Canadian writers I know hope that their work would in some way empower and educate.

REFERENCES

Baker, H.A., Jr. 1980. *The Journey Back: Issues in Black Literature and Criticism.* Chicago: University of Chicago Press.

Bell, D. 1992. *Faces at the Bottom of the Well: The Permanence of Racism.* New York: Basic Books.

Emmanuel, James A. 1971. "Blackness Can: A Quest for Aesthetics." In *The Black Aesthetic*, edited by Addison Gayle. New York: Doubleday.

Hill, L. 2001. *Black Berry, Sweet Juice.* Toronto: Harper Flamingo Canada.

Raabe, W. n.d. "Abraham Lincoln to Harriet Beecher Stowe: 'The author of this great war.'" https://wraabe.wordpress.com/2008/06/26/abraham-lincoln-to-harriet-beecher-stowe-the-author-of-this-great-war/

Shelley, P.B. 1967. "A Defence of Poetry." In *English Romantic Writers*, edited by David Perkins. New York: Harcourt.

Wordsworth, W. 1967. "Preface, Second Edition of the Lyrical Ballads." In *English Romantic Writers*, edited by David Perkins. New York: Harcourt.

A PICTURE OF WORDS

— ANGELA WALCOTT —

On August 9, 2017 I faced a bittersweet moment. I had to part ways with something that I felt was a part of me for a long time, but something that was never really mine to begin with. Travelling 222 miles, the visit would include a four-week stay in my hometown of Toronto for the summer. As the final hours approached, I had to agree with Sister Bradley, "I done got my feet caught in the sweet flypaper of life." And I was dogged if I wanted to shake loose.

got the call that my library material was ready for pick-up three days ago. There were no renewals allowed and it was recommended that I collect the item ASAP. "I'm here to pick up an interlibrary loan," I blurted to the librarian in a high-pitched tone. I did a power walk to end all power walks from the parking lot so I was slightly out of breath; a little sweaty but extremely excited. Embracing my inner geek, I felt I was on a mission—a mission that was long overdue. The librarian paused momentarily, disappeared behind a book trolley and retrieved a thin grey book in a matter of seconds. It looked unassuming. A large piece of paper taped around the front rendered me incapable of judging this book by its cover. "Where is the library book from?" I queried as I surrendered my library card.

The librarian stopped his paper-shuffling long enough to leaf through a few pages of the bound text before settling on the inside back cover page. Looking up, he smiled ever so slightly and said, "North Bay."

I don't recall hearing much about North Bay. All I know is that it's way up north and too far away from home. The one thing I do recall hearing a lot about was this book, *The Sweet Flypaper of Life*. It was first brought to my attention several years ago. I set the thought aside, but it was reintroduced to my psyche repeatedly. A lecture at the Royal Ontario Museum made mention of it. *One day*, I said.

Award-winning photographer and special guest lecturer Dawoud Bey mentioned the book again while lecturing at Ryerson University. *Another day*, I said.

And this goes on for a bit, until one day I decide on a whim, it's now or never. I fill out a form. *It doesn't really matter if it's now*, I thought, *I'd be waiting on never.*

I examine the book when I get home. A large white and yellow band of paper that says, 'Please Do Not Remove' securely encircles the front cover. Please Do Not Remove. *Christmas has come early*, I think to myself as I lift the paper flap ever so slightly, in the hopes that I can adequately judge this book by its cover. Over the next few days I begin to obsess with what is on the inside. I pour over its content like I have never done with a book before: drawing diagrams, taking notes and analyzing the positioning of words. But mostly, I celebrate. I celebrate the fact that I have a chance to experience this tactile literary jewel, if only for a short while. I even celebrate the sweet scent of 'old book.' First published in 1967, Langston Hughes and Roy DeCarava collaborated to create *The Sweet Flypaper of Life*, a tender depiction of African-American lives.

Roy DeCarava, an award-winning photographer/artist and the first African-American Guggenheim Fellow, together with Langston Hughes, legendary poet, novelist, and essayist, was a match made in creative, literary heaven. Their artistic genius provides a new perspective. Despite wrestling with a voyeuristic tendency of the book's images to peer into the kitchens and parlours of America's cross-section in this Harlem neighbourhood, we are made to feel welcome.

Nestled amongst the pages are striking images and striking words—words that string images together so thoughtfully and cohesively you wouldn't suspect that they were random. Hughes eloquently paints with words while DeCarava sculpts with film. Pictures and words equally consider one another. Told from the unique perspective of an African-American senior citizen, Sister Bradley is our trusted guide. Frame after frame, as the astute narrator shares her dreams we begin to understand her fears. In a pseudo-photo album delivered via DeCarava's work, Hughes flips the lens wide open by using ekphrastic writing to create an emotional connection with the reader. Ultimately, the artistic duo sheds light on Sister Bradley's life and the collective lives of countless African-Americans living during those tumultuous times in an important way. *The Sweet Flypaper of Life*, Sister Bradley. Upon receiving a telegram from the Lord to come home, Sister Bradley knows she isn't ready, because of the Supreme Court decree for integration. She wants to see what it will be like. *Sweet Flypaper* is a testimony to the everyday lives of everyday people in a not-so-ordinary world. Langston Hughes bravely delivers a timely, convincing narrative that confronts issues revolving around race, equality, family, and community in a beautiful way. It is a time not too long ago and not too often seen. African-Americans were ready for integration in a society that wasn't quite ready for them. It's not just a fancy case study report justifying the need for integration; this is a poignant example of the power of family and community told through pages. *The Sweet Flypaper of Life* is a photo album that helps to bear witness—its black-and-white photos leap from the page in full colour.

America's culturally rich tapestry unfolds from its Harlem suburb. The peeling paint of New York apartments where stoops substitute for balconies, represents an undeniable visual splendour. And yet amongst the still beauty is the urgency of its message, just as palpable today as it was when first written back in 1955. America was at the height of bridging its deep racial divide. Hughes deciphers this intersectionality via words while DeCarava helps us to see them. It's a glimpse into the 'everyday'—everyday lives told, but seldom seen.

At City Hall, in downtown Toronto, a multicultural oasis full of interesting people calls to me. Inside Nathan Phillips Square, I timidly accept this invitation and look out at the stage before me. The vast sea of grey doesn't appeal on this matching neutral day. I need contrast. I need repetition. I need texture. I need people. Everyone here has a story, but how can I weave a common thread in a convincingly *Sweet Flypaper* kind of way? Is it my duty?

Does the responsibility even lie with me?

Centre front: The Toronto sign, erected to mark the 2015 Pan Am Games hosted by 'The Six,' beckons. A group of eager tourists recline amongst the *O's*, while laughing children play against *T's* and too-cool Millennials pose for selfies in-between. I adjust my depth of field, hoping to capture something, anything. In this moment I intrude. In playback, the image is far from perfect.

Stage right: A lone lady with a large, red sun hat occupies a corner bench. I peer and play back. Still far from perfect. To the left, a woman walking her dog enters the frame from stage left. Her sparkly silver bunny shoes bedazzle. Snap. It looks okay.

Photography is about the connection. Roy de Carava invites his audience to explore the inner confines of far-removed worlds. After a forty-five-minute session shooting basketball players at 'Golden Hour,' I, the amateur, have collected over 200 random images. Would Roy DeCarava have shot this many in one session? Not. Twenty-four frames per roll were all you got. Each shot had to count. Determine the correct depth of field. And snap. Had I kept to this plan, my hard drive would not have housed thousands of so-so images. Not understanding the correct angle, shooting of the same subject from all possible angles became an obsession. It was a time-consuming, costly lesson of learning via trial and error. Because of this, I never dumped the bad shots. Hundreds of pictures grew into thousands. The more I took, the more compelled I would feel. I ignored the virtual reels of film gathering at my feet. I feared letting go would lead to missing out on the story.

Photography, like many realms of art, can occur 'by accident' or it can happen with a sense of purpose crafted by the careful planning of a story. My style tends to be the former. I stick to tight shots—abstractions of the truth. Today's assignment involves photographing people.

It's not something that I have explored before and, to be quite honest, it's unnerving. I'm not one for exploiting for the sake of the shot, but candid is one clear way of telling the truth.

Centre Stage: Sandwiched between the Toronto sign and the City Hall building, a young girl dressed in black leotards, pink tutu, and matching pink pointe shoes sails into an arabesque. Her wavy black hair, neatly coiled high atop her head in a tight bun, is the only thing that remains stationary. She gracefully pirouettes and ends with a grand gesture of jetés. A middle-aged Black woman is taking pictures of the ballerina girl. Her camera is similar to mine. I soon discover that this photographer is the ballerina's mom. We start talking. Mom is taking promotional shots of her daughter, who is studying at the National Ballet School. I ask permission to take a photo.

Mom and daughter smile. Mom agrees. I pace myself. Focus. Adjust the shutter speed. Now click. I hold my breath as I analyze the picture. There's a clearer story there. I see the truth.

In order to tell better stories as writers, we are instructed to show but not tell. *Sweet Flypaper* manages the subtle art of showing while telling. The collaborative, stunningly effective dialogue that erupts between writer and photographer is undeniable. Sometimes the artists switch places. While Hughes shows, DeCarava tells.

As I flip through the pages of *The Sweet Flypaper of Life* again, I see how Hughes quiets issues of contention with soothing prose. He reshapes and moulds a space into shared action. The stillness of DeCarava's images, both seemingly posed and candidly shot, presents a believable narrative. I see the duality of picture and words and I am moved even further. I get it. I venture through areas of my neighbourhood with a different perspective. My camera becomes the third eye. Vast worlds shrink into manageable bite-sized pieces. Fragments of colour, repeating lines, and defined shapes emerge from the woodwork. I discover that nothing is really ever planned when it comes to photography. Yes, planning how you want to deliver the story is something you prepare for ahead of time, but what enters the frame at any given moment is beyond your control.

Sometimes you have to trust, and when nothing goes according to plan, sometimes you just have to believe.

Despite my camera telling me otherwise, the day was an underwhelming mid-tone grey. Most of the photos I had been taking did not feature people—they featured landscapes and objects or abstractions of people.

I remember driving home from Thornhill. It was one of the foggiest nights on record, and despite the fact that I wanted to get off the road because visibility was reduced to nil, I wanted to stay. I didn't have my camera on hand, but I knew that it would make a great shot. I see photo opportunities in the strangest of places now: in my food, on subway walls, between nooks and crannies. Everywhere.

On August 9, I celebrated in my own way. I read and re-read *The Sweet Flypaper of Life* from beginning to end and I gave thanks for this gift before sending it all the way back to North Bay. North Bay is really far away from home, but maybe I could take my camera for a visit one day.

DEMAND SPACE

— *Chelene Knight* —

"But you don't look *that* Black."

I remember walking into an event where I was asked to be a guest reader by a woman who'd "heard about my book." We'd never met. I was unfamiliar with the other readers, had never heard of the venue, but was still interested in expanding my literary horizons. This is what emerging writers need to do, right? I introduced myself to her and she stared back at me for a good fifteen seconds before furrowing her brow and saying, "But you don't look *that* Black." I stood there, frozen in my purchased-especially-for-this-event black pumps, my mind spinning and fumbling for the appropriate reply. Once again I was left feeling less-than, not worthy of being part of the event because—according to the white organizer—I didn't fit the mould of what Black should be. I wasn't Black enough. How the hell is a Black person not Black enough? Simple. I didn't meet the expectations of the diversity hashtag. I knew I should have said something right then and there, but although I felt my mouth open, no sound was audible.

This was my initial attempt at navigating a mostly white-privilege-paved terrain (and I survived), but now imagine peeling back that first layer of not belonging, only to reveal another layer of still not belonging, thinner and less opaque, but another layer nonetheless. My mother is an American-born Black woman. My father is an East Indian-Ugandan who was forcefully removed from his country for *not* being Black, due to the violence, conflict, and displacement that took place in Uganda in the seventies. This unimaginable experience is obviously not comparable to being scrutinized at a literary reading, but having our skin colour be the deciding factor on how we are treated, is. I never grew up with my father, I never sat down with him and discussed how to handle situations where I was judged or made to feel less than. But just having the knowledge of what he has been through has taught me a few things. You can be born into a place, live there your whole life, and still never truly be home.

Home. A word that, to me, holds many definitions. The first, a physical place with doors, windows, a roof. The second, a feeling of contentment, safety, and belonging. I wanted both definitions. My family constantly told me that I was light-skinned and prettier because I had good hair. To this day I still have no idea what good hair is or should be.

But I remember feeling like all of the things that were intended to be compliments also made me the outsider. While everyone was inside the house—talking, eating, laughing—I was on the outside peering through the window, waiting for someone to open the door and welcome me in wholeheartedly.

Back at the reading I stood to the side of the wood-paneled podium, shifting my weight from one leg to the other. I tried to look like I knew what I was doing, so I turned the pages of my very first book with shaky fingers and I watched the words jump and blur. I was left to question my own Blackness in a room full of white people, with all eyes on me. I walked up to the mic and I felt my insides drop.

There's really no other way to describe it. Everything inside me fell to my feet and I was transported back to being eleven and some punk kid at school telling me I should pick a side, or my family telling me I had good hair and that I should be happy I am mixed.

This event was no different. They wanted me to pick a side. I fumbled through my reading without ever looking up from my book.

That one reading changed me. It split me in two. The first me is comfortable in her skin, doesn't feel the need to explain her own ethnicity, while the second me comes to the table orally armed, ready to defend myself as soon as the slightest pebble of doubt is tossed at my feet.

I constantly think about what it feels like to occupy one body that is essentially your own, but as two separate people: a Black woman writer and a writer. For one, it's extremely difficult to write while constantly bouncing back and forth like this. Walking into a literary reading to a full house where you are the only non-white face will always bring up questions: Am I the physical representation of a diversity hashtag? Is my writing good? Can I read to this particular room of people? What should we do going forward? We need to demand space.

Rush-hour commutes are similar wherever you go, but there will always be at least one person not willing to play by the rules, or even be the slightest bit considerate. The doors of a sardine-packed train open and the usual stuff-your-body-in-where-you-can game begins. I find a spot to wedge in and place my bag on the floor between my legs to make room for the person beside me and so that I'm not constantly slapping my purse against them every time the train jolts forward.

While on the train, I started to think about the space around me. I made do with what I had, while at the same time standing uncomfortably still as to not disturb those around me. There was no space to hold on because one very entitled woman thought the handrail dropped down from heaven just for her. She had the entire length of her arm against the yellow pole, so that the people on either side of her were forced to tilt and fall over multiple times as the train lurched to its abrupt stops. She looked straight ahead without moving.

Did she need the entire pole? No. Could she have moved, readjusted, so that the rest of us could grab onto a small part of the pole so that we wouldn't fall over? Yes. Did she consider this? No.

If someone refuses to give you the space, you must demand it. Take it. I wedged my hand in-between the pole and her forearm, unaffected by the look of utter annoyance on her face. I gripped pole, taking only the space I required. She didn't move and kept the pressure against my hand.

In fact, she increased it. Both of us looking forward, holding space, as the train wobbled along its tracks. After three stops she finally released the pressure against my hand. Another hand quickly gripped the pole. All of us looking forward, the only acknowledgement was *not* falling over.

I recently listened to a radio interview where Shelagh Rogers had a brief conversation with Donna Bailey Nurse about how no one is paying attention to Black Canadian female writers.* Bailey mentions that, in the late nineties, we came onto the scene hot and heavy, and then—disappeared. These writers were acknowledged. What happened? I'll tell you what happened: we demanded space, took it, then let go. We cannot publish because we are constantly told, "there is no audience for these books," and that we are not marketable. I wonder if this is because of the diversity hashtag issue and how certain intersections are hot right now. It's an unavoidable situation, the labelling will occur, but I want under-represented writers such as myself to demand space. Demand space, and keep it. Hold on tight.

Are we wanted because our story is important? Will the appetite for diversity dwindle? What does it mean to be a Black writer while others question your work, your reasons for writing, and your colour even before you've begun to write? And who has the right to even ask?

My writing runs constant circles around these questions: who gets accepted into the literary world, who is left out, and who decides? There is a fine line between tokenism and offering up a platform for marginalized voices.

I want to be heard. But does that mean I need to scream louder than everyone else, or say something that no one else is saying, and defend it to death? While this is exhausting, through hard work, muscles form. Repeating a constant repetitive motion creates strength. It builds a confidence. And that confidence brings about trust. I'm learning we can't always question why we are being included or why we are not. That being said, we do need our allies, and allies need to understand what they should

---

* CBC Books: The Next Chapter, "Donna Bailey Nurse on black women writers."

be doing to create space *and* give us the tools we need to maintain such space. Simply placing a Black editor in a role where all her colleagues are white is not diversity; it's tokenism.

Ask her what she needs to be able to create more space *and* give her the tools to do it. Watch magic happen.

I've only recently started to demand space in my life, especially outside of the literary community. My partner is a white, middle-class male. I start with him. I demand my time to speak and I don't back down. I am fully engaged and just as participatory in conversations as he is. I do this in groups so that people can see and hear that I am there, I have opinions, stories, and value. There is indeed an audience for my words, because I demand it.

Pushing and elbowing my way in is not as easy as I wish it could be. Demanding space doesn't always work, and people won't always be as willing to step aside or ask the right questions. There are times where I close the door to my room and just cry from exhaustion. I do not think I am exhausted from just the work itself, but from the emotional toll it takes on my body. Sometimes I find myself sitting at my desk, a permanent slump fixed on my back, my eyes glazed over, and thinking, "What's the point?" The self-doubt doesn't always last long, but those few minutes are enough to bring me to tears. So for now, I choose to elevate and promote the voices I think are important. We have to start somewhere. We have to do the work.

Sometimes I picture myself in a ditch. I am beside my partner, but he is in a separate ditch. We cannot see each other, we can only hear each other. Our ditches are identical, except that he has a ladder that reaches to the top and I don't. It's going to be a lot harder for me to climb out. There will be dirt under my nails, scrapes on my knees, and I will definitely want to give up. I'll need to get really creative. It'll be tough as hell, but I'll have quite the story to tell, right? There will be an audience for that. Privilege or no privilege, I will climb out of that ditch, dirty, exhausted, and thirsty—but it'll be my resourcefulness that got me through.

Resourcefulness. This may just be the key to obtaining and keeping the space we deserve. I can think outside the box all I want, but until we can all work together as a unit, nothing will stick. Peeling back these layers has taught me to ask the right questions and recognize when the answers just weren't good enough. If I could go back to that initial reading knowing what I know now, I wonder what I would say? I can't be sure. But I know what I would have *done*. Demand better. Demand space. Then take it.

BLACK/ DISABLED/ ARTIST

— BRANDON WINT —

My name is Brandon Wint. I am Black. I am disabled. I am an artist. While I am aware that, socially, labels such as these often do as much to obscure the nuances of human identity as to clarify them, I am bound, in some inextricable way, to claim these three words for myself: Black, disabled, artist.

I must claim these identities for myself because, if I do not, I know the world will weaponize these words against me or bludgeon me with the culturally loaded weight of them until I am small, or invisible, or powerless. I know this because I was born Black. I am the son of two people who immigrated from the Caribbean as children—my mother from Barbados and my father from Jamaica—in the early 1970s and found themselves in the sprawling, complicated expanse of a place, a mostly white place, called Toronto.

They, like all of the Black Caribbean immigrants of their generation, found themselves navigating not only the obvious, common struggles of immigrant experience—differences in culture, accent, language, and climate—but also this thing that was, for each of them, long before they ever met or became my parents, a ubiquitous challenge: intense race consciousness.

In the countries they had come from, Blackness was accepted, commonplace, and understood. In Canada, however, their Blackness, in addition to their accents and particularities of culture, marked them as 'other,' as outsider, as alien, and as threat. Perhaps, at the same time, being new to this place, they did not fully understand this strange, thinly veiled scrutiny. Perhaps, as only young children (my mother aged nine and my father twelve), they could not fully comprehend the intensity of the new gaze they found themselves under while walking the hallways at school or trying to connect with their classmates. But they felt it, just as I felt it in my own adolescence, and as I still sometimes feel it now.

This, I know, is Canada's DNA imposing itself on the racialized body, the alienated subject of its whims. Canada is, after all, a place that still sees itself as a white, settler colony, a strapping young disciple of colonial Europe's good breeding. It is no wonder, then, that my parents found themselves cold, shivering, and confounded not only by Canada's harsh December winds, but by the equally chilly, equally pervasive coolness of Canadian affections and attitudes.

I was born in this country, in the late summer of 1988, and raised in a place, Thornhill, Ontario, of palpable, though apparently well-meaning, Whiteness. Though the Thornhill of my youth was not full of explicit, unmitigated racial vitriol, I nonetheless felt the particular, invisible tension of moving my young, Black body through spaces—playgrounds, classrooms, malls, grocery stores, relationships—that expressed, in their subtle ways, the cultural dominance of Whiteness. I felt it in the way that the girls in my classes would gather around me and rub my head, calling me 'fuzzy wuzzy,' marvelling, collectively, at my tightly curled strands of hair that, when touched, produced a texture they had never felt before. I felt it in the way that such marvelling and objectification was always easier than genuine connection; always more convenient, somehow, than understanding my Blackness as part of an expression of a full, deep and beautiful humanity. So often, though, the gaze and expression of Whiteness does not accord Blackness the room to embody a full range of humanity. Instead, Blackness, by which I really mean beautiful, intelligent, complex, and resilient African-descendant people, is broken down into consumable parts. For centuries, on this continent and others, our bodies, our cultures, our artistic expressions have been ogled and appraised by Whiteness. Only rarely, however, has the Black body emerged from these appraisals without being psychically, emotionally, or physically dismembered. As a child I wondered, as I still wonder now, at the possibility of being Black and whole in the presence of a Whiteness that does not know how to keep its hands to itself.

If my Black body cannot help but feel the gaze of Whiteness calling it 'other,' then this body, for being both Black and disabled, is absolutely riddled with the wounds of other people's glances and judgments. Perhaps even more than Black skin, the visible expression of physical disability is met with shock, scorn, fear, and derision. As someone who was born with cerebral palsy, the question "Why do you walk like that?" has been posed to me more often than any other single question. The question, which might seem mostly benign at first, is not usually one of mild or innocent curiosity. It asks: What happened? What's wrong? and, Why are you here?

The first question can be answered rather simply. My cerebral palsy, as best as I can guess, exists as an outcome of my complicated situation at birth. I was born nearly two months prematurely; neither doctors, nurses, nor my own parents were fully prepared for when I arrived on September 13, 1988. Maybe something happened. I can't really say. The question of what's wrong with me is even simpler. The answer is: absolutely nothing.

It is the third question that I feel the impact of most strongly. When able-bodied people encounter my unique, swaying gait, or note the way my right foot tends to drag rather than lift when I walk, some of them want to know why I am in their presence. They want to know this because the world is understood to be an able-bodied world. Largely, cities, schools, sidewalks, and institutions of all sorts are built with only the 'able' body in mind. Ours is a world constructed to privilege able-bodied people almost to the point of the complete erasure of disabled ways of being and knowing. This is why, when some people (particularly children, who have, by nature, experienced less of the world) see me in public, they begin to wonder, in very literal ways, how it is I came to occupy the same space as them. They wonder this because, of all bodies, the disabled body is perhaps the least thought of, the least accounted for. It is the body that, among all others, is the most directly and literally marginalized.

They mean this question another way, too. In the case of someone like me, who embodies an unmistakable passion, curiosity, love, and enduring will to live, the question can take on a voice which says, implicitly: what audacity is it that makes you dare to dream, love, desire, and live in a world that says disabled people are less entitled to virtue than other people? I answer this question with every authentic expression of my being, and I respond to it most resoundingly in my poetry.

Ever since entering the national spoken word community in 2009, it has been important for me to understand how my life-long experiences as a disabled person have shaped the lens through which I understand the world, myself, and my capacities as an artist. The interrogation of the relationship between my disability and my artistry is so nuanced, so interwoven with the deepest parts of me, that it will probably be a perpetual source of intrigue, insight, and re-evaluation. Nonetheless, a few answers have revealed themselves to me in the process.

I believe that my disability, in combination with my race and the social context in which I was raised, made me the subject of an intense and persistent gaze. As a child, I was always aware of being seen. I was always aware of being reckoned with and (mis)understood according to the complexities of my physicality. Poetry writing developed in me, I think, as a way of looking back at the world and meeting its many gazes with my own robust subjectivity.

Poetry, therefore, has been as much a tool of resistance in my life as it has been one of introspection. As a now nearly-thirty-year-old man, the acts of writing and speaking are still the primary modes by which I assert my capacity for intellect, joy, sagacity, and self-awareness.

My career as a spoken word artist feels at once like a sublime gift and a worthy inheritance. It is a gift because a full-fledged career in poetry is always at least a little bit perilous, uncertain, or full of rigour. To have a livelihood in an art form as obscure as spoken word poetry is a distinct and uncommon blessing. Yet, in another very real sense, my artistic trajectory feels like an inevitable outcome of the unique identities I inherited at birth. If one is to live a dignified, passionate, fulfilling life as a Black man in a discreetly white supremacist society, one must be at least a little bit audacious. Likewise, if one is to prosper as a full-time disabled artist in a place where ableism is quotidian, one must have the sort of self-belief that naturally resists the often-limited societal understanding of disabled life. Being a Black disabled artist means that I assert, as a way of life, at least two layers of righteous audacity and temerity. While it is impossible to know for sure, it feels reasonable for me to say that, without the realities of my Blackness and my disability to propel me towards it, the path of an artist, poet, and public speaker might never have occurred to me. As it is, the life of a spoken word poet, in the way that it combines writing, speaking, and an unambiguous form of embodied self-presentation, is the necessary culmination of the resilience I've expressed in my lifetime as a Black, disabled person. It is through spoken word poetry that I claim and reclaim the possibility of being, at once, Black, disabled, and fully embodied. This is absolutely essential to the fruition of my full, glorious humanity. I cannot be fully, authentically alive unless there is space for me to claim all three. My life is devoted, subtly and explicitly, to carving out this space and existing brilliantly within it.

ABOUT THE **AUTHORS**

Fatuma Adar is a Somali-Canadian from Toronto who is passionate about sharing stories that centre the African diaspora. She won a Creative Writing Scholarship at the University of Saskatchewan, was long-listed in 2016's CBC Creative Nonfiction prize, and has been profiled in CBC's "Up Close: Young Black Women Making Canada Better." In 2017, she was in New York as a part of the The Bars Workshop at The Public Theatre, is a member of Obsidian Theatre's Playwrights Unit and is a Musical Stage Company's RBC Apprentice.

Shammy Belmore is a mixed-race artist from Alberta. They identify with both Indigenous and Somalian backgrounds and has a lot to say about their experiences being a racial minority in Canada.

Simone Blais is a young mixed-race woman who is based out of Toronto, Ontario, and Victoria, British Columbia. She is a dancer, poet, and student at the University of Victoria. Simone is also a full-spectrum doula and sex educator. Her work focuses on providing care for racialized and Indigenous folks and decolonizing popular ideas about sex and reproductive health.

Wenzdae Brewster is an eighteen-year-old university student, activist, and two-time business owner living in Toronto, Ontario. Wenzdae is a member of the Georgian Bay Métis Nation of Ontario and is Arawak/ Bajan from the island of Barbados.

Whitehorse, Yukon, has been **Christina Brobby**'s home for many years. Her essays have appeared in print and online publications. She is currently at work on a memoir. When she's not writing, Christina works at telling stories through the medium of photography.

Simone Makeba Dalton lives and writes in Toronto, where she's pursuing a creative writing MFA at the University of Guelph. Her work appears in *The Unpublished City* (BookThug), a mini anthology featuring eighteen of Toronto's emerging voices curated by Dionne Brand for International Festival Of Authors and its Toronto Lit Up series. Simone was born and raised in Trinidad and Tobago.

Méshama Rose Eyob-Austin is not your typical teenager, she's the epitome of #BlackGirlMagic! As an aspiring singer-midwife, her intention is to use her voice to make people feel. She has been featured on CBC's award-winning series "Real Talk on Race," she had her poem published by Community Contact, and she has won a public speaking prize for her take on #BlackLivesMatter vs. #AllLivesMatter. As an honour student with a number of awards under her belt, she isn't afraid to use her voice to speak up on important issues such as gendered violence. She starred in, co-produced, and co-directed a film for the Third Eye Collective using Ntozake Shange's powerful poem "With No Immediate Cause." Like the women before her who've inspired her (Nina Simone, Erykah Badu, her mother), it's the love that she has for Black women and future generations that motivates her to end unnecessary suffering.

Kyla Farmer is a transdisciplinary artist, intersectional economist, and arts professional based out of Toronto, Ontario. She is founder/owner of Oxum Creative and of Bredren Creative—artist and business solutions firms. In all that she does, Kyla combines social and environmental justice with her profound interest in the stories of her own ancestries and of those around her, fostering a community driven by a collective understanding of one another. She tells stories in community with literature—essays, poetry and prose. Kyla is also an award-winning filmmaker, producer, and curator.

Scott Fraser is a Toronto-based acquisitions editor at Dundurn Press. The first major influence on his thoughts as a Black person was Steve Biko, and he's been subsequently inspired by the work of C.L.R. James, Cornel West, and James Baldwin. When he's not working, he enjoys being involved with softball as a player, manager, and umpire, and writing occasionally. His work has also appeared in *Blood & Bourbon*.

Whitney French is a writer, storyteller, and multi-disciplinary artist. She's been published in a couple of places, but she takes more pride in the community she builds than in the things she produces. Whitney is also the founder and co-editor of the nation-wide publication, *From the Root Zine*, as well as the founder of the workshop series Writing While Black, an initiative to develop a community of Black writers. She is currently going through the painful process of writing her first science fiction novel. She is also the editor of this anthology.

Kaya Joan is an interdisciplinary artist who believes strongly in the power of creation to transcend. She draws inspiration from her surroundings and her ancestors. Kaya is working towards a Bachelor of Fine Art at OCAD University.

Chelene Knight is a Vancouver-born-and-raised graduate of The Writer's Studio at Simon Fraser University. In addition to being a workshop facilitator for teens, she is also a literary event organizer, host, and seasoned panellist. She has been published in various Canadian and American literary magazines, and her work is widely anthologized.

Chelene is currently the managing editor at *Room* magazine and the 2018 Programming Director for the Growing Room Festival. *Braided Skin*, her first book (Mother Tongue Publishing, March 2015), has given birth to numerous writing projects, including her second book, a memoir, *Dear Current Occupant* (BookThug, 2018). Chelene Knight is working on her third book, a novel about a friendship between two Black women who grew up in Vancouver (Hogan's Alley) in the 1930s and '40s.

Eternity Martis is a Toronto-based journalist and editor whose work has been featured in *Vice, Salon, Huffington Post, Broadly, xoJane, The Walrus,* TVO.*org,* CBC, CTV, *Hazlitt, Complex, The Fader, Canadaland,* and more.

Storyteller and chai lover, **Rowan McCandless** writes from Treaty 1 territory—the original lands of the Anishinaabe, Cree, Oji-Cree, Dakota, and Dene peoples, and homeland of the Métis Nation. An eighth-generation Africadian on her father's side, she won first place in *Room*'s 2017 Creative Nonfiction Contest and second place in *Room*'s 2015 Annual Poetry and Fiction Contest. Rowan also placed second in *Prairie Fire*'s 2016 Annual Fiction Contest and recently was longlisted for Prism International's 2017 Creative Nonfiction contest.

Mary Louise McCarthy is a seventh-generation woman of African descent from the province of New Brunswick. She received her BA in 1991 (York University), MEd in critical studies in 2007 (University of New Brunswick), and is currently working on her PhD in social justice (OISE, University of Toronto). In 2015, Mary Louise won a four-and-a-half-year battle through the Ontario Human Rights Tribunal where her case of racial profiling was successful. Mary Louise's doctoral research is dedicated to the early African settlers of New Brunswick and she is highlighting their lives, experiences, and subsequent segregated deaths.

Phillip Dwight Morgan is an emerging journalist, poet, and essayist of Jamaican heritage. His poetry and articles have appeared on *macleans.ca, cbc.ca,* and *rabble.ca,* as well as in *Briarpatch* and *Spacing* magazines. Born and raised in Scarborough, Ontario, Phillip uses writing to explore questions of race, representation, identity, and belonging in a Canadian context. Phillip views writing as a process of self-discovery, emancipation, and nourishment.

Délice Igicari M. Mugabo completed her MSc in geography, urban and environmental studies at Concordia University. Her work explored anti-black Islamophobia and the history of Muslim Black activism in Montreal in the 1990s. Currently a PhD student at The Graduate Center, City University of New York, her doctoral research examines the violence and punishment enslaved Black women fought against in seventeenth- and eighteenth-century Québec.

Chayo Moses Nyawello is a member of the Canadian Armed Forces, Department of National Defence, Reserve 4CRPG in Coy, BC. A former cab driver, Chayo now owns and runs a small business with his business partner, Mr. Patrick Watson: North Coast Transportation, ACTA-INC.

Christelle Saint-Julien is a Montreal-born and -based writer, musician, and translator. A hyperactive brainard, her first love really is music. She makes a living putting words together in different contexts.

Cason Sharpe is a writer born in Toronto and currently based in Montreal. His work has appeared in *Canadian Art, C Magazine*, and PRISM *International*, among others. He is the author of *Our Lady of Perpetual Realness and Other Stories* (Metatron, 2017).

Makeda Silvera is a Caribbean-Canadian lesbian feminist who was the publisher and managing editor of Sister Vision Press for sixteen years, from its inception in 1985 to its closing in 2001. Sister Vision Press was a groundbreaking, award-winning press, both nationally and internationally. Silvera is also an activist and author. Silvera's essays and short stories have appeared in many publications. She also tutored at York University's Writing Centre for many years.

H(ubert) Nigel Thomas was born in St. Vincent and now lives in Montreal, Canada. He is a retired professor of American literature and the author of ten books and dozens of essays. His novels, *Spirits in the Dark* (1993) and *No Safeguards* (2015), were shortlisted for the Quebec Writers Federation Hugh MacLennan Fiction Prize. In 2013, he was awarded Université Laval's Hommage aux créateurs. His novel *Behind the Face of Winter* (2001) and short story collection *Lives: Whole and Otherwise*

(2010) have been translated into French. He is the founder and principal coordinator of Logos Readings.

Angela Walcott is a multidisciplinary artist who aims to reshape the canvas with a unique sensibility that combines visual and written storytelling in nuanced ways. She has written reviews for various publications including *Maple Tree Literary Supplement*, *Public Journal*, THIS, and *Canadian Children's Book News*. Her artwork and photography have been exhibited at YYZ Gallery, Project Gallery, El Space, and the Skylight Gallery. She is the author of the children's picture book *I Want To Be*.

Brandon Wint is a poet, spoken word artist, and organizer currently living in Edmonton, Alberta. He is interested in using the potential of his poetry in combination with his physical potential as a Black, disabled person to tell stories of deep personal meaning and to situate himself sturdily in our complex world. He is a former Canadian poetry slam champion and a lover of poetic expression, wherever and however it can be found.

Sapphire Woods is a queer nerd with a passion for Black education and a nurturer of Black joy! Holding her masters of education, she plans on creating Black-youth-focused curricula through graphic novel education and transformative justice. Sapphire's positive obsessions are with Afrofuturism, graphic novels, being a plant mom, and eating ice cream.

Angela Wright is a writer and performance artist based in Toronto. Her creative nonfiction has appeared in *The Fiddlehead*, *The New Quarterly*, and *The Brooklyn Quarterly*. She also works in politics and her political commentary has appeared in *Maclean's*, *Toronto Star*, CBC *Opinion*, *Montreal Gazette*, *Torontoist*, and *Overland Literary Journal*. She is currently working on a personal memoir of a young woman who reflects on her childhood after experiencing hate crimes.

Rachel Zellars is a mother, professor, and co-founder of Third Eye Collective, the first organization in Montreal to support Black women who are survivors of gender-based violence. Originally a farm girl from upstate New York, she has lived in Montreal, Quebec, since 2015.

Printed by Imprimerie Gauvin
Gatineau, Québec